# 2D Game Collision Detection

An introduction to clashing geometry in games

Thomas Schwarzl

Copyright © Thomas Schwarzl, 2012

All rights reserved

ISBN-10: 1479298123
ISBN-13: 978-1479298129

# Table of Contents

## Introduction ... 1
- Features of This Book ... 1
- You Will Need ... 1
- You Won't Need ... 2
- Share Your Thoughts ... 2

## Atoms of Geometry: Vectors ... 3
- What Vectors Are ... 3
- Additions ... 5
- Scaling ... 8
- Length ... 10
- Null Vector ... 12
- Unit Vector ... 12
- Rotation ... 13
- Dot Product ... 17
- Projection ... 20

## Shapes ... 23
- Line ... 23
- Line Segment ... 25
- Circle ... 26
- Rectangle ... 27
- Oriented Rectangle ... 28

## Collision Detection ... 29
- Rectangle-Rectangle Collision ... 30
- Circle-Circle Collision ... 31
- Point-Point Collision ... 32
- Line-Line Collision ... 33
- Line-Segment-Line-Segment Collision ... 35
- Oriented-Rectangle-Oriented-Rectangle Collision ... 38
- Circle-Point Collision ... 42

| | |
|---|---|
| Circle-Line Collision | 43 |
| Circle-Line-Segment Collision | 44 |
| Circle-Rectangle Collision | 45 |
| Circle-Oriented-Rectangle Collision | 47 |
| Rectangle-Point Collision | 48 |
| Rectangle-Line Collision | 49 |
| Rectangle-Line-Segment Collision | 50 |
| Rectangle-Oriented-Rectangle Collision | 52 |
| Point-Line Collision | 56 |
| Point-Line-Segment Collision | 57 |
| Point-Oriented-Rectangle Collision | 58 |
| Line-Line-Segment Collision | 59 |
| Line-Oriented-Rectangle Collision | 60 |
| Line-Segment-Oriented-Rectangle Collision | 61 |

## Bounding Shapes ... 63

| | |
|---|---|
| Bounding Rectangle | 64 |
| Bounding Circle | 64 |
| Circle or Rectangle? | 65 |

## Shape Grouping ... 67

| | |
|---|---|
| Bounded Shape Groups | 67 |
| The Code | 68 |

## Shapes in Motion ... 71

| | |
|---|---|
| The Tunneling Problem | 71 |
| Linear Impact Search | 72 |
| Binary Impact Search | 73 |
| When Both Objects Move | 77 |

## Optimization Tricks ... 79

| | |
|---|---|
| Abstraction is King | 79 |
| Size Matters | 80 |
| Rotating by Right Angles | 80 |
| Pass Arguments by Reference | 81 |
| Avoid Square Root | 82 |

Short-Circuit Coding ................................................................. 82
Avoid Superfluous Tests ............................................................ 84
Level of Detail ............................................................................ 85

## Appendix: The Code ......................................................... 87

## About the Author ............................................................. 88

# Introduction

Are you curious how 2D collision detection in games works? If so this book is made for you.

In case you don't know what collision detection is: it's the determination of whether objects simulated in programs collide. This is a basic feature of computer games, e.g. for determining shot impacts, finding out which enemies are covered by lines of sight, recognizing collisions of race cars or simply checking if the mouse cursor floats above a button.

The book is written for game developers but is suited for other coder species as well.

## Features of This Book

This book was written with the following intentions in mind:

- be aimed at beginners,
- use successive knowledge building,
- leverage ´a picture paints a thousand words´,
- provide working code,
- allow it to also function as a reference book and
- enable fast navigation by cross-linking

This book has less than 100 pages. That's not much for a textbook. Nonetheless, that's intentional. Serving up the necessary information on a minimum of pages is better than throwing a 500+ page tome at you. Brevity is the soul of wit.

## You Will Need

... knowledge in basic procedural programming. All code is written in the language

C. C is the "mother" of modern imperative programming languages. So the language choice for this book was a no-brainer. If you're more familiar with C++, Java, Objective-C or C# you won't have any problems understanding what's going on in this book.

The code was written for comprehensibility. Some details were simplified or left out to get short and understandable code. Therefore the book's code may not be 100% correct C code.

Further there are no optimizations or fancy tricks in the code. That would compromise understandability.

Check out the appendix, which provides all code from this book as a download.

## You Won't Need

... an academic degree. As long as you understand addition, multiplication and can read equations you should not encounter any problems throughout this book.

Oh, wait! You'll need to know what a square root is.

And what's *PI*.

I'm afraid elementary school children are out. Sorry.

## Share Your Thoughts

If you have any questions about the book, collision detection or programming in general just drop me a line. Critique, praise and professional curses are welcome as well:

*thomas@collisiondetection2d.net*

I'm looking forward to hearing from you.

# Atoms of Geometry: Vectors

Game objects need physical representations. Games use diverse geometric shapes for this. To find out if two objects collide we just have to check if their shapes intersect.

In computer games shapes usually get described by vectors. They are the building blocks for shapes and collision detection. So we first have to understand vectors and what we can do with them before we can tackle shapes and collision detection.

## What Vectors Are

In 2D space a vector is simply a displacement in two dimensions. Vectors have length and direction but no position. A simple definition for 2-dimensional vectors is:

*A 2D vector describes a straight movement in 2D space.*

The two dimensions are called X and Y. The following illustration and code shows exemplary 2D vector *v*:

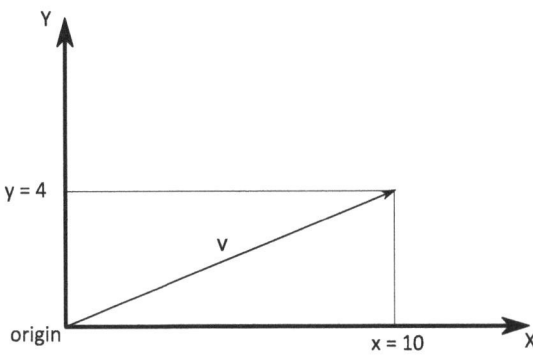

```
typedef struct
{
    float x;
    float y;
} Vector2D;

Vector2D v = {10, 4};
```

The black arrows represent the coordinate system aka 2D space. The horizontal arrow illustrates the X-axis of the coordinate system, the vertical one illustrates axis Y. Their shared starting point is called the *origin*. The position of the *origin* is always *{0, 0}*.

> We will use notation *{x, y}* for vectors throughout the whole book. It's the same notation used for initializing vectors in code. Examples for this notation are *{10, 4}, {-208, 13}* or *{0, -47.13}*.

Vector *v* goes from the *origin* 10 units along axis X and 4 units along axis Y. Using our vector notation:

*v = {10, 4}*

This is the very same expression you can find in the code example above.

The vectors *origin* and *v* can also be seen as points in the coordinate system. The words *point* and *vector* are interchangeable in this case.

## Additions

Vector addition can be imagined as chaining vectors. As mentioned in the preceding section, a vector is a displacement in 2D space. Let's assume we have point *a*, add vector *b* and get the resulting point *c*:

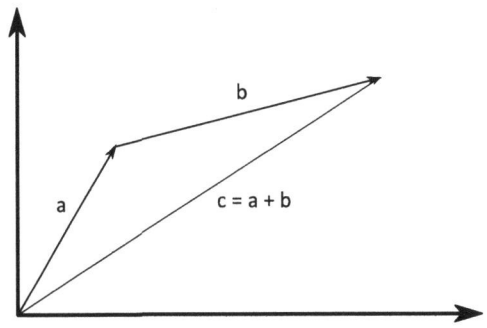

```
Vector2D add_vector(Vector2D a, Vector2D b)
{
    Vector2D r;
    r.x = a.x + b.x;
    r.y = a.y + b.y;
    return r;
}

Vector2D a = {3, 5};
Vector2D b = {8, 2};

Vector2D c = add_vector(a, b);
```

Vector *c* points to the position which vector *a* points to after it is displaced by vector *b*. This displacement is known as vector addition or, in math tongue, vector translation.

Now that we know how vector addition works, what about vector subtraction? Subtraction is as simple as addition:

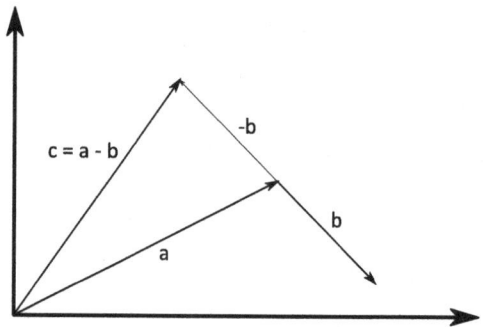

```
Vector2D subtract_vector(Vector2D a, Vector2D b)
{
    Vector2D r;
    r.x = a.x - b.x;
    r.y = a.y - b.y;
    return r;
}

Vector2D a = {7, 4};
Vector2D b = {3, -3};

Vector2D c = subtract_vector(a, b);
```

Subtraction can also be seen as adding a negated vector. In our case it would be adding negative *b* to *a*:

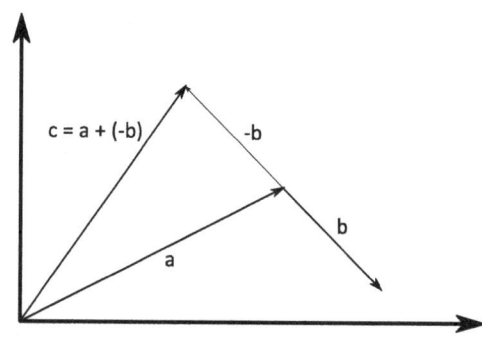

```
typedef enum { no = 0, yes = 1 } Bool;

Vector2D negate_vector(Vector2D v)
{
    Vector2D n;
    n.x = -v.x;
    n.y = -v.y;
    return n;
}

Bool equal_floats(float a, float b)
{
    float threshold = 1.0f / 8192.0f;
    return fabsf(a - b) < threshold;
}

void assert_equal_vectors(Vector2D a, Vector2D b)
{
    assert(equal_floats(a.x, b.x));
    assert(equal_floats(a.y, b.y));
}

Vector2D a = {7, 4};
Vector2D b = {3, -3};

Vector2D c = add_vector(a, negate_vector(b));

assert_equal_vectors(c, subtract_vector(a, b));
```

This code needs a little bit of explanation. First data type *Bool* is defined. It has just two possible values: *yes* and *no*. Any logical statement will return one of these two values.

> If you're familiar with C you may ask: "Why not use well known *true* and *false*?". The terms *yes* and *no* were adopted from Objective-C because they are more readable.

Function *negate_vector()* should be self-explanatory: it takes a vector and returns it pointing in the opposite direction.

Function *equal_floats()* and *assert_equal_vectors()* are test functions. The former returns *yes* when the two parameters are equal. The latter checks if two vectors are equal. If not, function *assert()* is used to signal an error.

> Functions *equal_floats()*, *assert_equal_vectors()* and *assert()* will often be used throughout the book. The basic function *assert()* - which experienced coders surely know – takes the result of an assertion as a parameter. If the assertion is true the function does nothing. If it's wrong the function signals a problem, e.g. showing a small message box stating an error message. Function *assert()* is just used to verify that a result is as expected.
>
> Function *equal_floats()* takes two float values and returns *yes* if they are **nearly** equal. You may be puzzled why we can't just write $a == b$. The problem with floats is that they suffer from rounding errors. Tiny deviations already break code like $a == b$. Therefore we have to be more tolerant and test the difference of *a* and *b* to be below a certain threshold. For this we use the function *fabsf()* - a C standard function - which returns its parameter's absolute value. In other words it returns the parameter without its sign.

Finally $a - b = a + (-b)$. Vector addition (which includes subtraction) works the same way as addition of simple numbers.

## Scaling

Scaling a vector is done by multiplying the vector's two values *x* and *y* with a number. In this case the number is called a scalar:

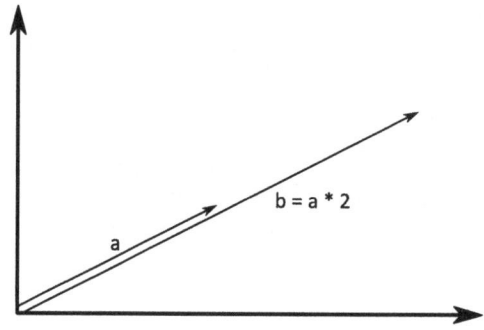

```
Vector2D multiply_vector(Vector2D v, float scalar)
{
    Vector2D r;
    r.x = v.x * scalar;
```

```
    r.y = v.y * scalar;
    return r;
}

Vector2D a = {6, 3};
Vector2D b = multiply_vector(a, 2);

assert(equal_floats(b.x, 12));
assert(equal_floats(b.y, 6));
```

Scaling can change only a vector's length and not its direction.

Where there is multiplication there is also division. As you may guess it's about dividing the vector's values by a number, in this case called a divisor:

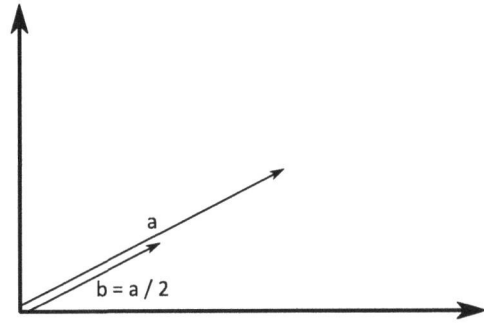

```
Vector2D divide_vector(Vector2D v, float divisor)
{
    Vector2D r;
    r.x = v.x / divisor;
    r.y = v.y / divisor;
    return r;
}

Vector2D a = {8, 4};
Vector2D b = divide_vector(a, 2);

assert(equal_floats(b.x, 4));
assert(equal_floats(b.y, 2));
```

Division can also be seen as a multiplication by *1/divisor:*

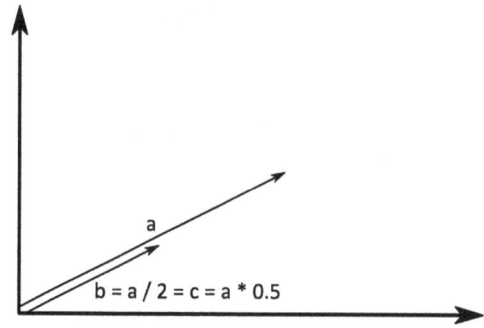

```
Vector2D a = {8, 4};
float divisor = 2;

Vector2D b = divide_vector(a, divisor);
Vector2D c = multiply_vector(a, 1 / divisor);

assert_equal_vectors(b, c);
```

Finally, the following scenarios exist in vector scaling:

- *scalar > 1*: the vector gets longer
- *scalar = 1*: the vector stays the same
- *0 < scalar* and *scalar < 1*: the vector shrinks
- *scalar = 0*: the vector becomes *{0, 0}*, it points nowhere!
- *scalar < 0*: the vector points in the opposite direction

## Length

The length of a vector is the distance from its origin to its tip.

The Pythagorean theorem is well suited to calculating a vector's length. It says that in a triangle with side lengths *a*, *b* and *c* and a right angle between *a* and *b* the following equation is always true:

$c^2 = a^2 + b^2$

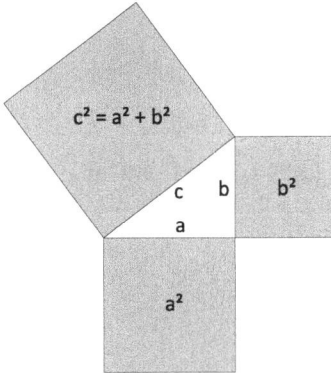

When we use this theorem for vectors we can imagine $a$ as $x$ and $b$ as $y$. This way $c$ is equal to the vector's length. Rearranging the equation for $c$ gives us this formula:

$c = squareroot(a^2 + b^2) = length = squareroot(x^2 + y^2)$

We just have to write this equation as code:

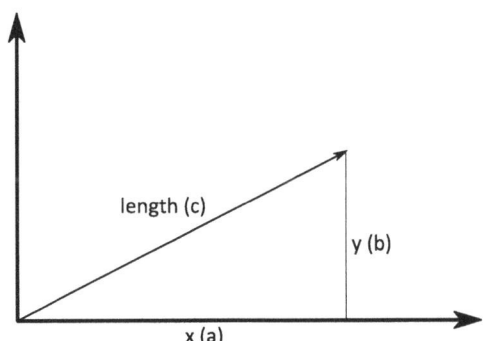

```
float vector_length(Vector2D v)
{
    return sqrtf(v.x * v.x + v.y * v.y);
}

float a = 10;
float b = 5;
Vector2D v = {a, b};
float c = vector_length(v);
```

Function *sqrtf()* is a C standard library function that computes the square root of a value.

## Null Vector

The null vector is *{0, 0}*. Logically it has a length of zero.

End of story.

## Unit Vector

A unit vector is any vector with a length of 1. Examples would be *{0, 1}*, *{-1, 0}* or *{0.7071, -0.7071}*.

You get unit vector *u* from vector *v* by simply dividing *v* by its length. Both vectors *u* and *v* point in the same direction but (may) have different lengths:

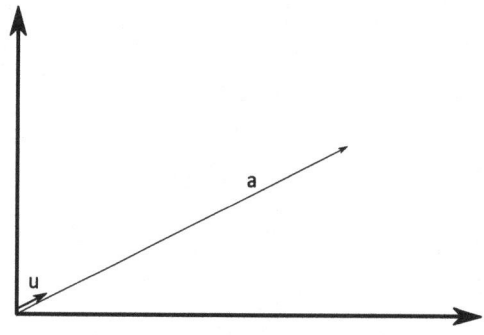

```
Vector2D unit_vector(Vector2D v)
{
    float length = vector_length(v);
    if(0 < length)
        return divide_vector(v, length);
    return v;
}

Vector2D a = {10, 5};
assert(1 < vector_length(a));

Vector2D u = unit_vector(a);
assert(equal_floats(1, vector_length(u)));
```

There is a special case: the null vector *{0, 0}*. The length of the null vector is zero so calculating its unit vector would include a division by zero, which is undefined. In this case the result is the null vector itself.

In which direction does a "point" point anyway?

## Rotation

Vector rotation changes the direction in which a vector points. In this operation the vector's length stays the same. Just its orientation changes.

The common unit for angles is degree where 360 degrees describe a full rotation. In programming it's different - here angles get measured in radians. A full rotation equals *2 * PI* radians which is about 6.283. So 360 degrees are equal to *2 * PI* radians.

Despite radian being the unit of choice for programming, we will use the renowned degrees. For most people it's not intuitive that 1.5708 radians describe a right angle. On the other hand an angle of 90 degrees (= 1.5708 radians) is well known for this. As said before this book should be easy to understand, not academically sophisticated.

Throughout the rest of this book the degrees symbol ° will be used. For example 120 degrees will be written as 120°. Just to give you a one up on where these little "O"s come from.

OK, enough explanation. Let's get started with vector rotation:

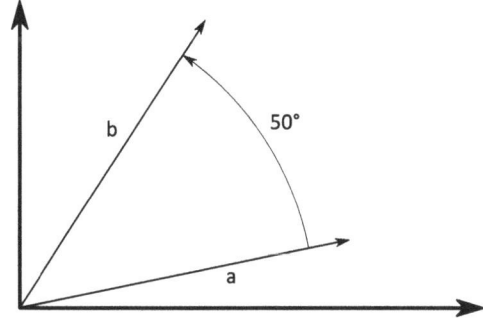

```
float degrees_to_radian(float degrees)
{
    float pi = 3.14159265358979323846f;
    return degrees * pi / 180.0f;
}

Vector2D rotate_vector(Vector2D v, float degrees)
{
    float radian = degrees_to_radian(degrees);
    float sine = sinf(radian);
    float cosine = cosf(radian);

    Vector2D r;
    r.x = v.x * cosine - v.y * sine;
    r.y = v.x * sine + v.y * cosine;
    return r;
}

Vector2D a = {12, 3};
Vector2D b = rotate_vector(a, 50);
```

Rotation is more complex than translation or scaling. There's some trigonometry and angle unit conversion involved. The latter is needed because the C standard library functions *sinf()* and *cosf()* want their angles in radians. This is the point where the above mentioned degree/radian relation comes into play.

To understand rotation we need to have a look at the unit circle. This special circle is centered at position *{0, 0}* and has radius 1, hence the name:

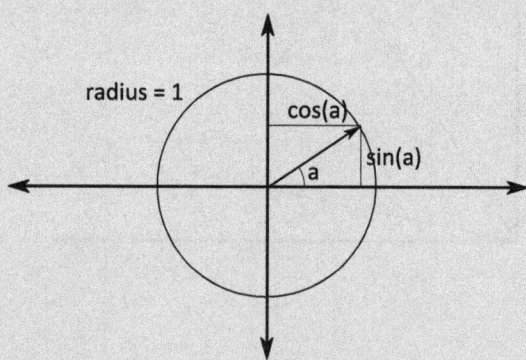

Any point on the circle can be described as vector *{1, 0}* rotated by an angle *a*. This vector is a unit vector because its length is 1. The illustration shows how to rotate unit vector *{1, 0}* by angle *a*:

(1) *rotate_unit_x(a) = (cos(a), sin(a))*

We can use *rotate_unit_x()* for rotating any vector *v* which has *y* = *0*:

(2) *rotate_vector(v, a) = v.x * rotate_unit_x(a)*

This is the first step for rotating an arbitrary vector. The next step is to find a formula for rotating the upwards-pointing unit vector *{0, 1}*. This can be achieved by rotating unit vector *{1, 0}* by angle *a + 90°*:

(3) *rotate_unit_y(a) = rotate_unit_x(a + 90) = (cos(a + 90), sin(a + 90))*

According to trigonometric rules we can convert the equation into this form:

(4) *rotate_unit_y(a) = (cos(a) * cos(90) − sin(a) * sin(90),*
                       *cos(a) * sin(90) + sin(a) * cos(90))*

Expressions *sin(90)* and *cos(90)* are constants and can be replaced by *sin(90) = 1* and *cos(90) = 0*:

(5) *rotate_unit_y(a) = (cos(a) * 0 − sin(a) * 1, cos(a) * 1 + sin(a) * 0)*

The final, simplified definition for *rotate_unit_y()* is:

(6) *rotate_unit_y(a) = (− sin(a), cos(a))*

Using this function we can rotate any vector having *x* = *0*:

(7) *rotate_vector(v, a) = v.y * rotate_unit_y(a)*

Now we know how to rotate unit vectors *{1, 0}* and *{0, 1}* and their scales *{x, 0}* and *{0, y}*. The final step for rotating an arbitrary vector *v* is to split it into two perpendicular, coordinate-system-axes-aligned vectors, rotate them and recombine them to get rotated *v*:

(8) *v = {x, y} = {x, 0} + {0, y} = vx + vy*

Rotating these two vectors by angle *a* and adding them afterwards gives us *v* rotated by *a*:

(9) *rotate_vector(v, a) = rotate_vector(vx, a) + rotate_vector(vy, a)*

Here we can rewrite *vx* and *vy* using equations (2) and (7):

(10) *rotate_vector(v, a) = v.x * rotate_unit_x(a) + v.y * rotate_unit_y(a)*

Substitutions with (1) and (6) give us:

(11) *rotate_vector(v, a) = v.x * (cos(a), sin(a)) + v.y * (– sin(a), cos(a))*

A little rearrangement and we are done:

(12) *rotate_vector(v, a) = (v.x * cos(a) – v.y * sin(a), v.x * sin(a) + v.y * cos(a))*

That's how it goes.

Rotations by positive angles go counterclockwise. When the angle exceeds 360° (full circle) it wraps around. E.g. a rotation by 370° gives the same result as a rotation by 10°. In code this would be:

```
Vector2D v1 = rotate_vector(v, a);
Vector2D v2 = rotate_vector(v, a + 360);
assert_equal_vectors(v1, v2);
```

Negative rotations go clockwise. Due to the wrap-around nature of rotation we can substitute a negative angle with a positive one by adding a multiple of 360° until it becomes positive. E.g. a rotation by -40° gives the same result as a rotation by 320°.

It's important to mention that these rotation directions are true for coordinate systems where positive x expands to the right and positive y expands upwards. If, for example, positive x were to expand to the left then the rotation directions would switch.

## Dot Product

The dot product, also known as scalar product or inner product, is an abstract concept. It describes the relation between two vectors with a single number.

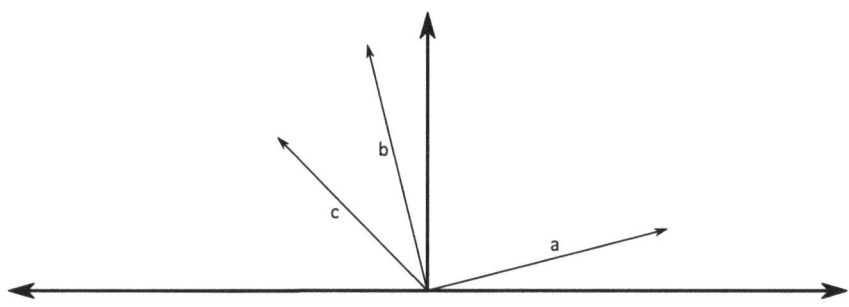

```
float dot_product(Vector2D a, Vector2D b)
{
    return a.x * b.x + a.y * b.y;
}

Vector2D a = {8, 2};
Vector2D b = {-2, 8};
Vector2D c = {-5, 5};

assert(equal_floats(0, dot_product(a, b)));
assert(0 > dot_product(a, c));
assert(0 < dot_product(b, c));
```

The code above shows that the dot product's algorithm is quite simple. But what do the results mean?

The following conditions reveal information about the enclosed angle:

- When the dot product equals zero the angle between the vectors is 90°.
- When the dot product is positive the angle is less than 90°.
- When the dot product is negative the angle is greater than 90°.

When you take a look at the illustration, vectors *a* and *b* share a right angle. Their dot product proves this: it's zero. Vectors *a* and *c* share an angle greater than 90° so their dot product is negative. Finally *b* and *c* enclose an angle less than 90° so their dot product is positive.

The dot product itself is an easy and cheap way to get an idea of the angular constellation of two vectors.

But there is more. We can calculate the actual angle between two vectors using the dot product in combination with their unit vectors.

Check this out:

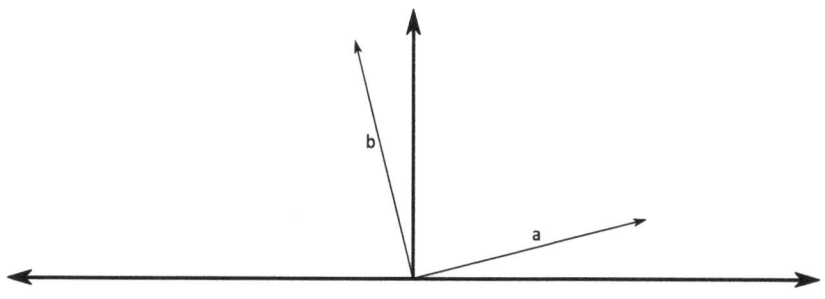

```
float radian_to_degrees(float radian)
{
    float pi = 3.14159265358979323846f;
    return radian * 180.0f / pi;
}

float enclosed_angle(Vector2D a, Vector2D b)
{
    Vector2D ua = unit_vector(a);
    Vector2D ub = unit_vector(b);
    float dp = dot_product(ua, ub);
    return radian_to_degrees(acosf(dp));
}

Vector2D a = {8, 2};
Vector2D b = {-2, 8};

assert(equal_floats(90, enclosed_angle(a, b)));
assert(equal_floats(0, dot_product(a, b)));
```

Pure magic, isn't it?

An important fact about the dot product:

(1) *dot_product(v1, v2) = cos(a) * length(v1) * length(v2)*

In this equation *v1* and *v2* are vectors and *a* is their enclosed angle. Transforming the equation for isolating *cos(a)* on one side gives us the following:

(2) *dot_product(v1, v2) / (length(v1) * length(v2)) = cos(a)*

The dot product allows this substitution:

(3) *dot_product(s1 * v1, s2 * v2) = s1 * s2 * dot_product(v1, v2)*

Combining (2) and (3) gives us this equation:

(4) *cos(a) = dot_product(v1 / length(v1), v2 / length(v2))*

From section Unit Vector we know that a vector divided by its length is its unit vector. Therefore we can rewrite (4) as follows:

(5) *cos(a) = dot_product(unit_vector(v1), unit_vector(v2))*

Now we just have to get rid of function *cos()* by applying its inverse operation arc-cosine on both sides of the equation:

(6) *acos(cos(a)) = acos(dot_product(unit_vector(v1), unit_vector(v2))) = a*

Finally we got the formula used in function *enclosed_angle()*.

The explanation why (1) is true is a little complex and has therefore been omitted. If you really want to know how this rule comes together check out Wikipedia's dot product page *http://en.wikipedia.org/wiki/Dot_product*.

There is one further useful detail. A vector's dot product with itself is its length squared:

*dot_product(v, v) = v.x² + v.y² = length²*

Squared vector lengths are often used in geometric calculations. The reason why is explained in section Avoid Square Roots.

## Projection

A projection is a vector mapped onto another vector. An illustration and some code should clarify the concept:

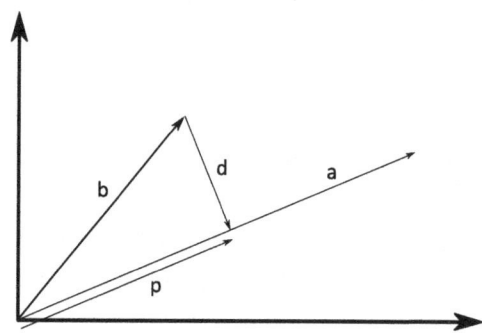

```
Vector2D project_vector(Vector2D project, Vector2D onto)
{
    float d = dot_product(onto, onto);
    if(0 < d)
    {
        float dp = dot_product(project, onto);
        return multiply_vector(onto, dp / d);
    }
    return onto;
}

Vector2D a = {12, 5};
Vector2D b = {5, 6};
Vector2D p = project_vector(b, a);
```

The result of projecting *b* onto *a* is *p*.

To deduce function *project_vector()* we combine three simple equations. The first is a trigonometric rule:

(1) *cos(a) = adjacent / hypotenuse*

In the vector projection illustration adjacent and hypotenuse are the lengths of *p* and *b*:

(2) *cos(a) = length(p) / length(b)*

This is the first equation we need. The second one comes from section Dot Product:

(3) *cos(a) * length(v1) * length(v2) = dot_product(v1, v2)*

In the vector projection illustration we substitute *v1* by *a* and *v2* by *b*:

(4) *cos(a) * length(a) * length(b) = dot_product(a, b)*

Replacing *cos(a)* in (4) with (2) gives this equation:

(5) *(length(p) / length(b)) * length(a) * length(b) = dot_product(a, b)*

We remove the neutralizing *length(b)* terms and resolve for *length(p)*:

(6) *length(p) = dot_product(a, b) / length(a)*

This is the second equation we need. The third and last equation is this:

(7) *unit_vector(p) = unit_vector(a) = p / length(p)*

We rearrange it to get *p* on one side:

(8) *p = unit_vector(a) * length(p)*

Finally we can substitute *length(p)* in (8) with (6):

(9) *p = unit_vector(a) * dot_product(a, b) / length(a)*

Getting rid of *length(a)* gives us better computational performance:

(10) $p = (a / length(a)) * (dot\_product(a, b) / length(a))$

(11) $p = a * dot\_product(a, b) / (length(a) * length(a))$

(12) $p = a * dot\_product(a, b) / dot\_product(a, a)$

That's how function *project_vector()* gets deduced.

# Shapes

After getting used to vector math it's time for the next level: geometrical shapes and their definitions.

We will investigate the following shapes in this book:

- lines,
- line segments,
- circles,
- axis-aligned rectangles and
- oriented rectangles

This chapter presents these different shapes and how to describe them in code. The next chapter will show you how to check them for collisions.

## Line

In collision detection lines are always straight. When they are curvy they are, well, curves.

A possible definition of line:

*A line is the shortest connection of two points with infinite distance.*

Huh? What does this mean?

Lines are straight and endless. Usually we consider a line to start at some point and stop at an other point. In geometry this is called a line segment. However lines extend infinitely in both directions.

In this book's code a line will be defined as a base point with a direction. The line goes through the point, infinitely heading in both the direction and its opposite direction.

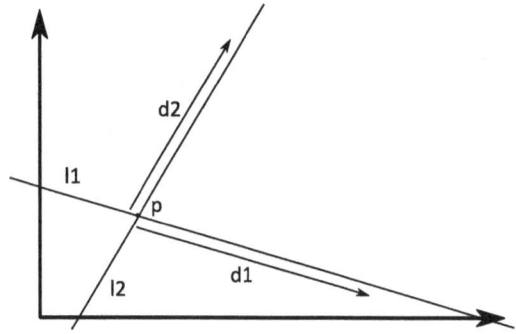

```
typedef struct
{
    Vector2D base;
    Vector2D direction;
} Line;

Vector2D p = {3, 3};
Vector2D d1 = {7, -2};
Vector2D d2 = {3, 5};

Line l1 = {p, d1};
Line l2 = {p, d2};
```

Because $p$ is the base point for both lines $l1$ and $l2$ they cross exactly at $p$. The upcoming section Line-Line Collision explains how to determine whether two lines intersect.

## Line Segment

Lines are straight and endless. But in collision detection we rather need lines to start at one point and end at an other point. This is called a line segment.

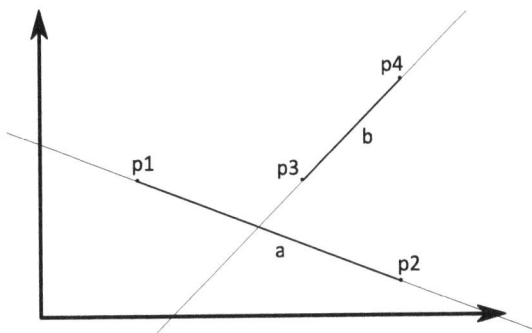

```
typedef struct
{
    Vector2D point1;
    Vector2D point2;
} Segment;

Vector2D p1 = {3, 4};
Vector2D p2 = {11, 1};
Vector2D p3 = {8, 4};
Vector2D p4 = {11, 7};

Segment a = {p1, p2};
Segment b = {p3, p4};
```

The two end points define the line segment. The code shows that the structure is named just *Segment* instead of *LineSegment*. The simple reason: the author is a lazy coder.

## Circle

Circles have a center point and a radius.

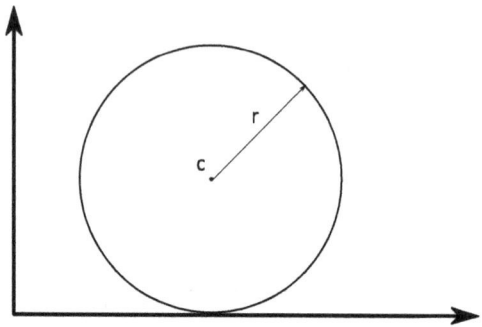

```
typedef struct
{
    Vector2D center;
    float radius;
} Circle;

Vector2D c = {6, 4};
float r = 4;

Circle a = {c, r};
```

The definition is as simple as the intersection algorithm. You will see in section Circle-Circle Collision.

## Rectangle

A rectangle is a shape with four sides where each corner has a right angle.

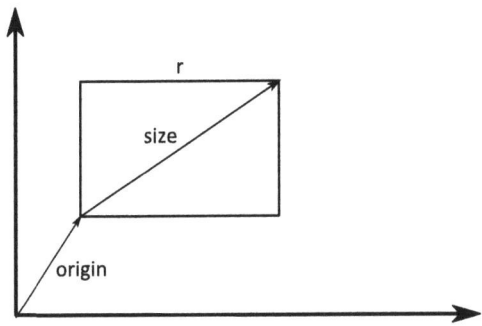

```
typedef struct
{
    Vector2D origin;
    Vector2D size;
} Rectangle;

Vector2D origin = {2, 3};
Vector2D size = {6, 4};

Rectangle r = {origin, size};
```

Usually rectangles are meant to have sides parallel to the coordinate system axes. So we are talking about axis-aligned rectangles.

## Oriented Rectangle

Oriented rectangles have, like axis-aligned ones, position and size. But they also have a rotation.

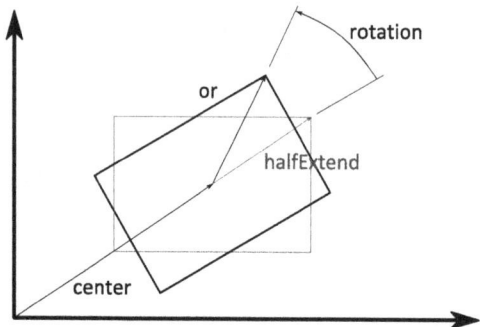

```
typedef struct
{
    Vector2D center;
    Vector2D halfExtend;
    float rotation;
} OrientedRectangle;

Vector2D center = {6, 4};
Vector2D halfExtend = {3, 2};
float rotation = 30;

OrientedRectangle or = {center, halfExtend, rotation};
```

For describing oriented rectangles we use the center instead of the origin and the rectangle's half extend (= half size) instead of the size. This pays off when we have to check them for intersections.

# Collision Detection

Finally we've arrived at chapter Collision Detection, the heart of this book. Now we get down to the nitty-gritty.

Collision detection answers a simple question:

*Do two shapes intersect?*

In its simplest form collision detection answers this question with just yes or no. The next question would be:

*How/where do the shapes intersect?*

This book focuses on the yes/no answers. That's enough for many 2D games.

Because there are different types of shapes, collision detection needs special functions for each possible pairing. We have 6 different shapes (including points) so we need 21 functions to cover all possible combinations.

First the homogeneous collision checks get explained, for example circle-circle, line-line, etc. Then we'll have a look at all the heterogeneous collisions like rectangle-point, circle-line, etc.

Fasten your seatbelt! The mental roller coaster ride starts now.

## Rectangle-Rectangle Collision

Collision detection for axis-aligned rectangles is really easy. We just have to check for overlaps in both dimensions.

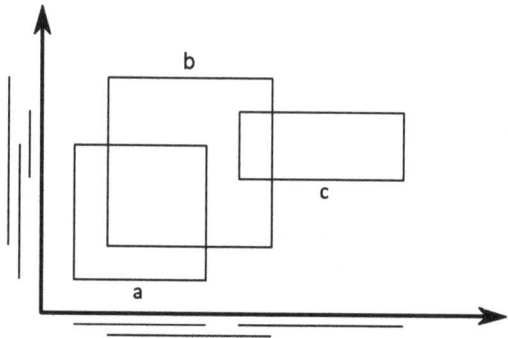

```
Bool overlapping(float minA, float maxA, float minB, float maxB)
{
    return minB <= maxA && minA <= maxB;
}

Bool rectangles_collide(Rectangle a, Rectangle b)
{
    float aLeft = a.origin.x;
    float aRight = aLeft + a.size.x;
    float bLeft = b.origin.x;
    float bRight = bLeft + b.size.x;

    float aBottom = a.origin.y;
    float aTop = aBottom + a.size.y;
    float bBottom = b.origin.y;
    float bTop = bBottom + b.size.y;

    return overlapping(aLeft, aRight, bLeft, bRight)
        &&
           overlapping(aBottom, aTop, bBottom, bTop);
}

Rectangle a = {{1, 1}, {4, 4}};
Rectangle b = {{2, 2}, {5, 5}};
Rectangle c = {{6, 4}, {4, 2}};
```

```
assert(yes == rectangles_collide(a, b));
assert(yes == rectangles_collide(b, c));
assert(no == rectangles_collide(a, c));
```

You can see the rectangle projections drawn along both coordinate system axes. The horizontal projections of *a* and *b* overlap. So do their vertical projections. Therefore rectangles *a* and *b* intersect. The same is true for *b* and *c*. Rectangles *a* and *c* overlap vertically but not horizontally. So these two rectangles can't intersect.

## Circle-Circle Collision

Two circles intersect when the distance between their centers is less than the sum of their radii.

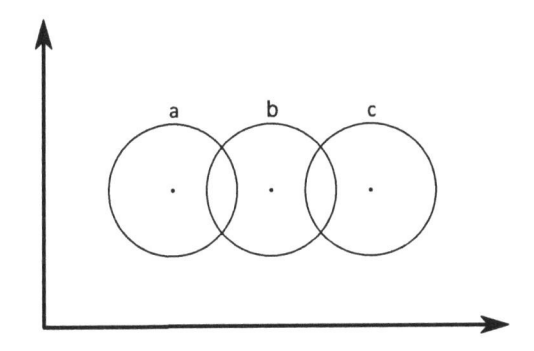

```
Bool circles_collide(Circle a, Circle b)
{
    float radiusSum = a.radius + b.radius;
    Vector2D distance = subtract_vector(a.center, b.center);
    return vector_length(distance) <= radiusSum;
}

Circle a = {{4, 4}, 2};
Circle b = {{7, 4}, 2};
Circle c = {{10, 4}, 2};

assert(yes == circles_collide(a, b));
assert(yes == circles_collide(b, c));
assert(no == circles_collide(a, c));
```

The centers of circle *a* and *b* are 3 units apart. Both circles have a radius of 2 units. Because the distance is less than the sum of the radii (3 < 4) *a* and *b* intersect. The same is true for *b* and *c*. The center distance of *a* and *c* measures 6 units. Too far apart for *a* and *c*'s radius 2 to intersect (6 > 4).

## Point-Point Collision

Determining point collision is trivial: two points intersect when they have equal coordinates.

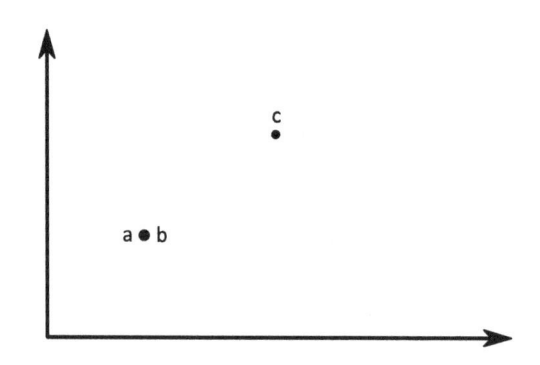

```
Bool points_collide(Vector2D a, Vector2D b)
{
    return equal_floats(a.x, b.x) && equal_floats(a.y, b.y);
}

Vector2D a = {2, 3};
Vector2D b = {2, 3};
Vector2D c = {3, 4};

assert(yes == points_collide(a, b));
assert(no == points_collide(a, c));
assert(no == points_collide(b, c));
```

Point-point collision detection is rarely used in games. Why? Imagine two soldiers firing their guns at each other. How likely would two bullets collide?

## Line-Line Collision

From section Line we know that lines are endless. So there are just two situations where lines don't collide: when they are parallel and not equivalent.

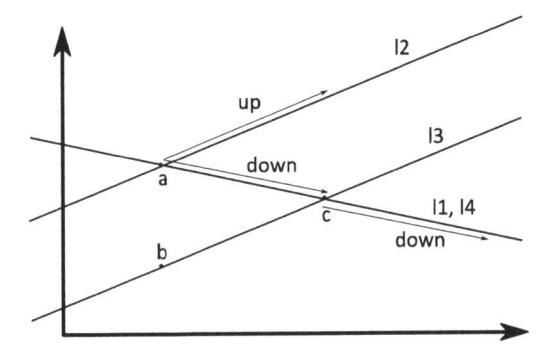

```
Vector2D rotate_vector_90(Vector2D v)
{
    Vector2D r;
    r.x = -v.y;
    r.y = v.x;
    return r;
}

Bool parallel_vectors(Vector2D a, Vector2D b)
{
    Vector2D na = rotate_vector_90(a);
    return equal_floats(0, dot_product(na, b));
}

Bool equal_vectors(Vector2D a, Vector2D, b)
{
    return equal_floats(a.x - b.x, 0)
           &&
           equal_floats(a.y - b.y, 0);
}

Bool equivalent_lines(Line a, Line b)
{
    if(!parallel_vectors(a.direction, b.direction))
        return no;

    Vector2D d = subtract_vector(a.base, b.base);
    return parallel_vectors(d, a.direction);
```

```
}

Bool lines_collide(Line a, Line b)
{
    if(parallel_vectors(a.direction, b.direction))
        return equivalent_lines(a, b);
    else
        return yes;
}

Vector2D a = {3, 5};
Vector2D b = {3, 2};
Vector2D c = {8, 4};

Vector2D down = {5, -1};
Vector2D up = {5, 2};

Line l1 = {a, down};
Line l2 = {a, up};
Line l3 = {b, up};
Line l4 = {c, down};

assert(yes == lines_collide(l1, l2));
assert(yes == lines_collide(l1, l3));
assert(no  == lines_collide(l2, l3));
assert(yes == lines_collide(l1, l4));
```

There are quite some functions involved in line collision detection. Let's go through it top-down.

As defined above only non-parallel or equivalent lines collide. Function *lines_collide()* first checks if the lines are parallel. If they are it returns their equivalence. Otherwise the lines collide so *yes* gets returned.

Function *parallel_vectors()* uses a simple trick to test vectors for parallelism. We know from section Dot Product that two vectors enclose a right angle when their dot product is zero. So when two vectors are parallel we just need to rotate one of them by 90° and check their dot product. That's exactly what *parallel_vectors()* does.

Instead of utilizing *rotate_vector()*, which takes arbitrary angles, we use the specialized function *rotate_vector_90()*. It's faster due to a simple trick which is explained in section Rotating by Right Angles.

A prerequisite for explaining *equivalent_lines()* is to know what equivalence means in this regard. There's a slight difference between *equal* and *equivalent*. Equal lines have the same base point and the same direction. One could be the clone of the other. Equivalent lines, on the other hand, just need parallel direction vectors and must have their base point somewhere on the other line. So line base and direction can be different from the other line's base and direction. Only the outcome, the drawn lines if you will, must be identical.

Function *equivalent_lines()* first tests for parallelism. If the lines are parallel we need to find out if the base point of one line lies on the other line. This is the case if the distance vector between the two base points is parallel to any of the lines.

## Line-Segment-Line-Segment Collision

For line segment collision checks we use a concept called "separating axis theorem". The SAT states:

*If there exists a line that separates two shapes they cannot intersect.*

Theoretically there is an infinite amount of possible axes. The best candidates in the case of line segments are the axes the segments go along.

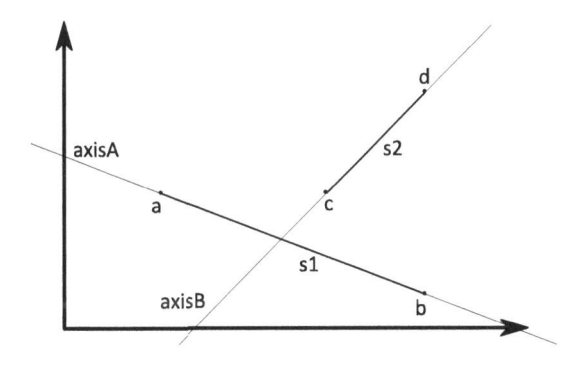

```
Bool on_one_side(Line axis, Segment s)
{
    Vector2D d1 = subtract_vector(s.point1, axis.base);
    Vector2D d2 = subtract_vector(s.point2, axis.base);
    Vector2D n = rotate_vector_90(axis.direction);
    return dot_product(n, d1) * dot_product(n, d2) > 0;
}

typedef struct
{
    float minimum;
    float maximum;
} Range;
```

```
Range sort_range(Range r)
{
    Range sorted = r;
    if(r.minimum > r.maximum)
    {
        sorted.minimum = r.maximum;
        sorted.maximum = r.minimum;
    }
    return sorted;
}

Range project_segment(Segment s, Vector2D onto)
{
    Vector2D ontoUnit = unit_vector(onto);

    Range r;
    r.minimum = dot_product(ontoUnit, s.point1);
    r.maximum = dot_product(ontoUnit, s.point2);
    r = sort_range(r);
    return r;
}

Bool overlapping_ranges(Range a, Range b)
{
    return overlapping(a.minimum,
                       a.maximum,
                       b.minimum,
                       b.maximum);
}

Bool segments_collide(Segment a, Segment b)
{
    Line axisA, axisB;
    axisA.base = a.point1;
    axisA.direction = subtract_vector(a.point2, a.point1);
    if(on_one_side(axisA, b))
        return no;

    axisB.base = b.point1;
    axisB.direction = subtract_vector(b.point2, b.point1);
    if(on_one_side(axisB, a))
        return no;

    if(parallel_vectors(axisA.direction, axisB.direction))
    {
        Range rangeA = project_segment(a, axisA.direction);
        Range rangeB = project_segment(b, axisA.direction);
        return overlapping_ranges(rangeA, rangeB);
    }
    else
```

```
        return yes;
}
Vector2D a = {3, 4};
Vector2D b = {11, 1};
Vector2D c = {8, 4};
Vector2D d = {11, 7};

Segment s1 = {a, b};
Segment s2 = {c, d};

assert(no == segments_collide(s1, s2));
```

Function *on_one_side()* returns *yes* when both end points of a (line) segment lie on the same side of a given axis. The following illustration shows the function's inner workings:

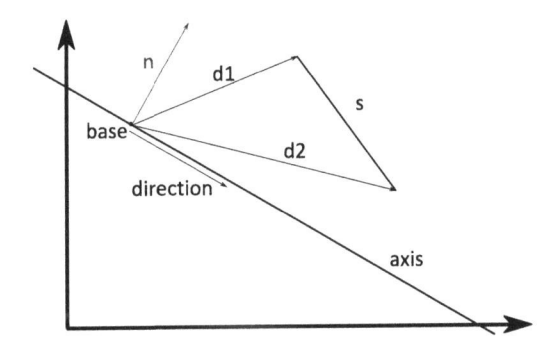

Vector *n* is perpendicular to (the) *axis*. If the dot products of *n* with *d1* and *n* with *d2* are both positive *s* completely lies on one side of *axis*. This is also true when both dot products are negative. If the dot product signs are different the segment crosses *axis*. Multiplication is a simple way to find out if two numbers have the same sign. If they do, the result is positive. When a dot product is zero the corresponding segment end point lies exactly on *axis*. This special case is interpreted as "not separating".

Function *segments_collide()* first interprets segment *a* as *axis* and tests if *b* lies on one side of it. If that's not the case (*axisA* intersects with segment *b*) the test is done vice versa: *b* defines the *axis* where segment *a* gets tested to lie on one side of it. If that's not the case either (*axisB* intersects with segment *a*) there is only one special case left to check: both segments lie on the same line (*axisA* = *axisB*) and overlap along this line. Here a few new functions come into play.

To find out if two parallel segments overlap we project them onto their shared axis and check the results. This is the same concept as used in function *rectangles_collide()*: the SAT. The difference is that the axis can be an arbitrary line. Therefore we need function *project_segment()* which projects a segment onto a vector, much like *project_vector()* does with vectors. The result is a *Range* that defines a one-dimensional area by its minimum and maximum. When the two projected segments (or more precisely their ranges) overlap we have detected a collision.

## Oriented-Rectangle-Oriented-Rectangle Collision

For oriented rectangles we use the SAT, just like we used it for line segments. We inspect the axes along all sides of both rectangles to find a separating one.

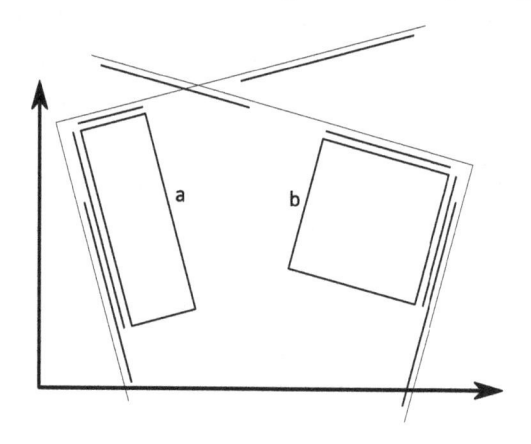

```
Range range_hull(Range a, Range b)
{
    Range hull;
    hull.minimum = a.minimum < b.minimum ? a.minimum :
                                           b.minimum;
    hull.maximum = a.maximum > b.maximum ? a.maximum :
                                           b.maximum;
    return hull;
}

Segment oriented_rectangle_edge(OrientedRectangle r, int nr)
{
    Segment edge;
    Vector2D a = r.halfExtend;
    Vector2D b = r.halfExtend;
```

```
    switch(nr % 4)
    {
        case 0:
            a.x = -a.x;
            break;
        case 1:
            b.y = -b.y;
            break;
        case 2:
            a.y = -a.y;
            b = negate_vector(b);
            break;
        default:
            a = negate_vector(a);
            b.x = -b.x;
            break;
    }

    a = rotate_vector(a, r.rotation);
    a = add_vector(a, r.center);

    b = rotate_vector(b, r.rotation);
    b = add_vector(b, r.center);

    edge.point1 = a;
    edge.point2 = b;
    return edge;
}
Bool separating_axis_for_oriented_rectangle(Segment axis,
                                            OrientedRectangle r)
{
    Range axisRange, r0Range, r2Range, rProjection;
    Segment rEdge0 = oriented_rectangle_edge(r, 0);
    Segment rEdge2 = oriented_rectangle_edge(r, 2);
    Vector2D n = subtract_vector(axis.point1, axis.point2);

    axisRange = project_segment(axis, n);
    r0Range = project_segment(rEdge0, n);
    r2Range = project_segment(rEdge2, n);
    rProjection = range_hull(r0Range, r2Range);

    return !overlapping_ranges(axisRange, rProjection);
}

Bool oriented_rectangles_collide(OrientedRectangle a,
                                 OrientedRectangle b)
{
```

```
    Segment edge = oriented_rectangle_edge(a, 0);
    if(separating_axis_for_oriented_rectangle(edge, b))
        return no;

    edge = oriented_rectangle_edge(a, 1);
    if(separating_axis_for_oriented_rectangle(edge, b))
        return no;

    edge = oriented_rectangle_edge(b, 0);
    if(separating_axis_for_oriented_rectangle(edge, a))
        return no;

    edge = oriented_rectangle_edge(b, 1);
    return !separating_axis_for_oriented_rectangle(edge, a);
}
OrientedRectangle a = {{3, 5}, {1, 3}, 15};
OrientedRectangle b = {{10, 5}, {2, 2}, -15};

assert(no == oriented_rectangles_collide(a, b));
```

Let's start with function *oriented_rectangles_collide()*. Its first test takes an edge (number 0) from rectangle *a* and tests if the axis along this segment separates the rectangles. If so, there can't be a collision. Otherwise the function takes the next edge (number 1) and repeats the test. If neither test finds a separating axis the two tests are repeated with edges from rectangle *b*.

Function *oriented_rectangle_edge()* returns the specified edge of a rectangle as a segment. It's not defined which edge will be returned for which number. It's only guaranteed that adjacent numbers correspond to connected edges. For example edges for numbers 0 and 1 share a corner point. The same is true for combinations 1-2, 2-3 and 3-0.

Function *separating_axis_for_oriented_rectangle()* is a special thing. It takes a segment (representing a rectangle edge) and a rectangle as parameters. The segment defines the axis that both parameters get projected onto. Have a look at the following illustration:

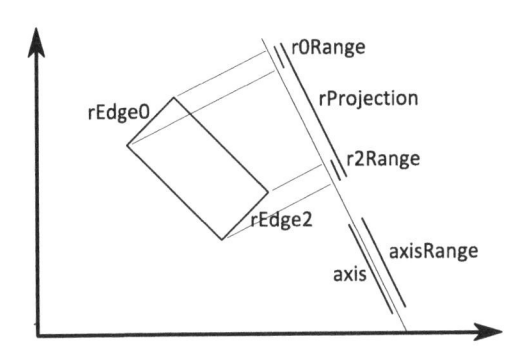

First we project two opposing rectangle edges onto the axis and name them *r0Range* and *r2Range*. Then we create their hull *rProjection*, the range which spans from the minimum of the two ranges to their maximum.

> It does not matter whether we use edges 0-2 or 1-3. It's just important that the edges are opposing. The resulting hull will be the same in both cases.

Finally we convert segment axis to range *axisRange*. In the illustrated example *rProjection* and *axisRange* don't overlap. Because segment axis is a rectangle edge we can say that the two rectangles can't intersect/collide.

## Circle-Point Collision

A point lies within a circle if the distance between circle center and point is less than the circle's radius.

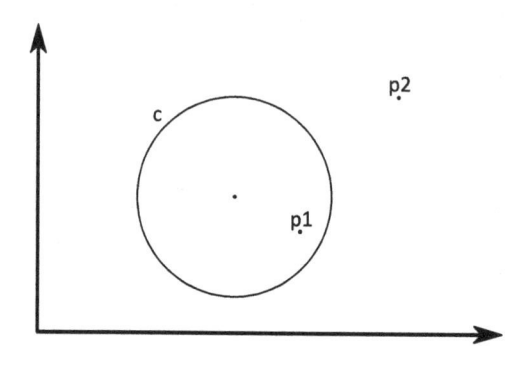

```
Bool circle_point_collide(Circle c, Vector2D p)
{
    Vector2D distance = subtract_vector(c.center, p);
    return vector_length(distance) <= c.radius;
}

Circle c = {{6, 4}, 3};
Vector2D p1 = {8, 3};
Vector2D p2 = {11, 7};

assert(yes == circle_point_collide(c, p1));
assert(no == circle_point_collide(c, p2));
```

This is the same concept as used for circle-circle collision. Replacing the points with circles having radius zero and using the circle-circle collision function would yield the same results.

## Circle-Line Collision

For this type of collision detection we first have to compute the point on the line which is closest to the circle's center. Then we test if this point lies within the circle.

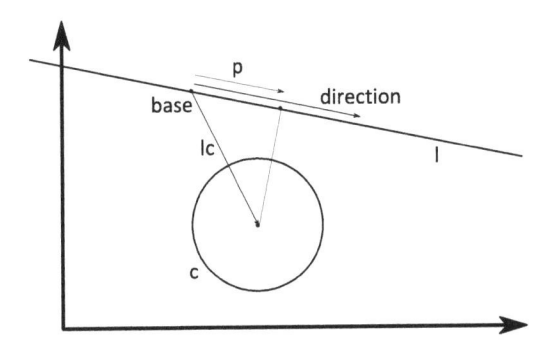

```
Bool circle_line_collide(Circle c, Line l)
{
    Vector2D lc = subtract_vector(c.center, l.base);
    Vector2D p = project_vector(lc, l.direction);
    Vector2D nearest = add_vector(l.base, p);
    return circle_point_collide(c, nearest);
}

Circle c = {{6, 3}, 2};
Line l = {{4, 7}, {5, -1}};

assert(no == circle_line_collide(c, l));
```

First the function calculates the distance vector *lc*, going from the line's base point to the circle center. Then it projects *lc* onto the line. The line's closest point to the circle center is *nearest*, the sum of *p* and the line' base point. When point *nearest* collides with the circle the line going through it does as well.

## Circle-Line-Segment Collision

In most collision situations between circle and segment at least one segment end point lies inside the circle. Therefore we check out these cases first. If both end points are outside the circle there is just one situation left where a collision is possible: the segment cuts through the circle.

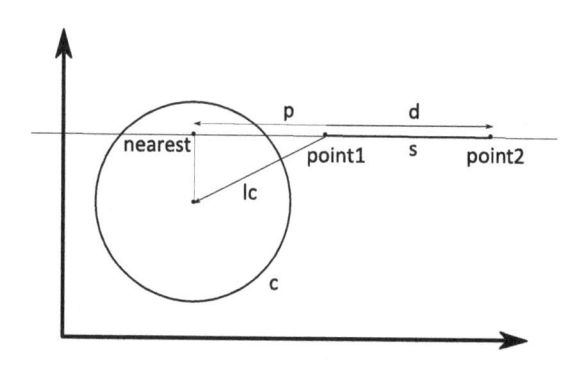

```
Bool circle_segment_collide(Circle c, Segment s)
{
    if(circle_point_collide(c, s.point1))
        return yes;
    if(circle_point_collide(c, s.point2))
        return yes;

    Vector2D d = subtract_vector(s.point2, s.point1);
    Vector2D lc = subtract_vector(c.center, s.point1);
    Vector2D p = project_vector(lc, d);
    Vector2D nearest = add_vector(s.point1, p);

    return circle_point_collide(c, nearest)
            &&
            vector_length(p) <= vector_length(d)
            &&
            0 <= dot_product(p, d);
}

Circle c = {{4, 4}, 3};
Segment s = {{8, 6}, {13, 6}};

assert(no == circle_segment_collide(c, s));
```

The first two tests in function *circle_segment_collide()* should be self-explanatory.

Afterwards comes the code which checks if the segment cuts through the circle. This code is an extended version of the circle-line collision code. The new parts are checking if *p* is shorter than *d* and if their dot product is positive. If *p* is longer than *d*, point nearest cannot lie on the segment. If the dot product is negative *p* and *d* are opposing and *nearest* lies outside of the segment.

The example in the illustration shows that none of the segment end points lie inside the circle. Point *nearest* lies inside the circle but it's off the line segment. Therefore a collision is not possible.

## Circle-Rectangle Collision

This collision detection can be simplified to a circle-point collision detection. We just need to find the point in the rectangle which is closest to the circle's center. If this point collides with the circle the rectangle does as well.

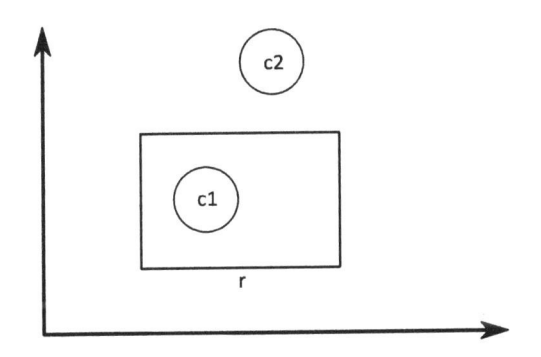

```
float clamp_on_range(float x, float min, float max)
{
    if(x < min)
        return min;
    else if(max < x)
        return max;
    else
        return x;
}

Vector2D clamp_on_rectangle(Vector2D p, Rectangle r)
{
    Vector2D clamp;
    clamp.x = clamp_on_range(p.x,
```

```
                        r.origin.x,
                        r.origin.x + r.size.x);
    clamp.y = clamp_on_range(p.y,
                        r.origin.y,
                        r.origin.y + r.size.y);
    return clamp;
}

Bool circle_rectangle_collide(Circle c, Rectangle r)
{
    Vector2D clamped = clamp_on_rectangle(c.center, r);
    return circle_point_collide(c, clamped);
}

Rectangle r = {{3, 2}, {6, 4}};
Circle c1 = {{5, 4}, 1};
Circle c2 = {{7, 8}, 1};

assert(yes == circle_rectangle_collide(r, c1));
assert(no == circle_rectangle_collide(r, c2));
```

Function *clamp_on_range()* returns the value between *min*(-imum) and *max*(-imum) with the least distance to value *x*. This is called clamping as the function name already suggests.

Analogously *clamp_on_rectangle()* clamps a vector on a rectangle. This is the two-dimensional equivalent of *clamp_on_range()*.

Finally *circle_rectangle_collide()* tests if the circle center clamped on *r* lies inside *c*.

## Circle-Oriented-Rectangle Collision

In case of collision detection between a circle and an oriented rectangle we use a simple trick: we transform both shapes into the rectangle's local coordinate system. This way we can use the function already explained for circle-rectangle collision detection.

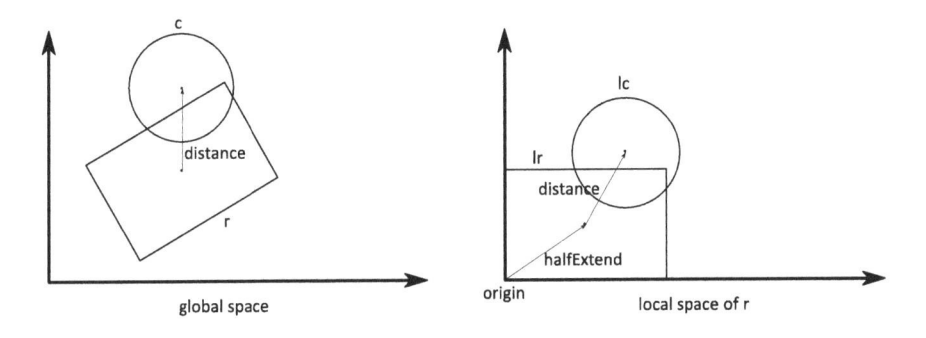

```
Bool circle_oriented_rectangle_collide(Circle c,
                                       OrientedRectangle r)
{
    Rectangle lr;
    lr.origin.x = 0;
    lr.origin.y = 0;
    lr.size = multiply_vector(r.halfExtend, 2);

    Circle lc = {{0, 0}, c.radius};
    Vector2D distance = subtract_vector(c.center, r.center);
    distance = rotate_vector(distance, -r.rotation);
    lc.center = add_vector(distance, r.halfExtend);

    return circle_rectangle_collide(lc, lr);
}
OrientedRectangle r = {{5, 4}, {3, 2}, 30};
Circle c = {{5, 7}, 2};

assert(yes == circle_rectangle_collide(c, r));
```

In the rectangle's local coordinate system the rectangle is called *lr* and the circle is called *lc*.

Defining *lr* should be obvious. The code says it all.

The center of *lc* is the sum of the center distance and the rectangle's half extend. To calculate distance we rotate the vector going from *r*'s center to *c*'s center by the inverse rectangle orientation. Inverse rotation means using the negative angle.

Now that everything is relative to *lr*'s origin we can use the circle-rectangle collision detection function.

> When oriented rectangles come into play we can use the function variants dealing with axis-aligned rectangles by transforming the shapes into the rectangle's local coordinate space.

## Rectangle-Point Collision

Determining if a point lies within a rectangle is easy:

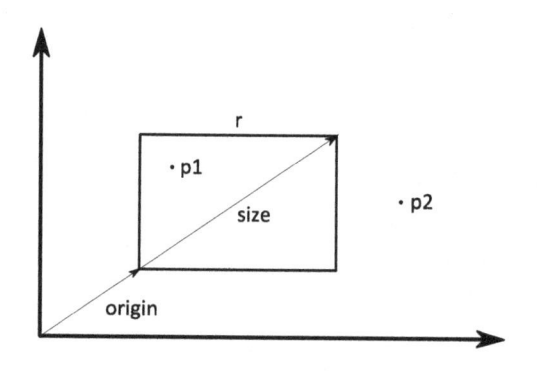

```
Bool point_rectangle_collide(Vector2D p, Rectangle r)
{
    float left = r.origin.x;
    float right = left + r.size.x;
    float bottom = r.origin.y;
    float top = bottom + r.size.y;

    return left <= p.x
           &&
           bottom <= p.y
           &&
           p.x <= right
```

```
            &&
            p.y <= top;
}

Rectangle r = {{3, 2}, {6, 4}};
Vector2D p1 = {4, 5};
Vector2D p2 = {11, 4};

assert(yes == point_rectangle_collide(p1, r));
assert(no == point_rectangle_collide(p2, r));
```

There should be nothing left to explain.

## Rectangle-Line Collision

A rectangle does not collide with a line if all corners of the rectangle are on one side of the line. This is the same concept as used for line-segment-line-segment collisions.

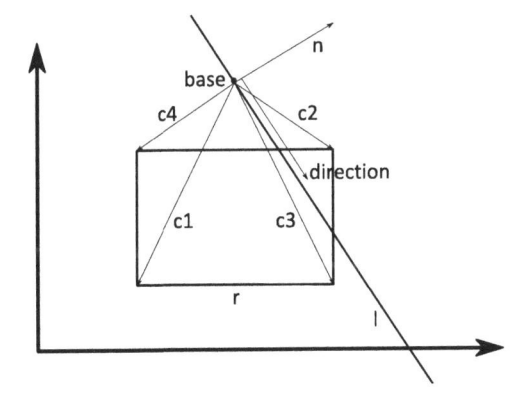

```
Bool line_rectangle_collide(Line l, Rectangle r)
{
    Vector2D n = rotate_vector_90(l.direction);

    float dp1, dp2, dp3, dp4;

    Vector2D c1 = r.origin;
    Vector2D c2 = add_vector(c1, r.size);
    Vector2D c3 = {c2.x, c1.y};
    Vector2D c4 = {c1.x, c2.y};
```

```
    c1 = subtract_vector(c1, l.base);
    c2 = subtract_vector(c2, l.base);
    c3 = subtract_vector(c3, l.base);
    c4 = subtract_vector(c4, l.base);

    dp1 = dot_product(n, c1);
    dp2 = dot_product(n, c2);
    dp3 = dot_product(n, c3);
    dp4 = dot_product(n, c4);

    return (dp1 * dp2 <= 0)
           ||
           (dp2 * dp3 <= 0)
           ||
           (dp3 * dp4 <= 0);
}
Line l = {{6, 8}, {2, -3}};
Rectangle r = {{3, 2}, {6, 4}};

assert(yes == line_rectangle_collide(l, r));
```

In the illustrated example, the angle between $n$ and $c2$ is less than 90°. Vector $n$ encloses, with $c1$, $c3$ and $c4$, angles greater than 90°. This means the dot product of $n$ and $c2$ is positive while the others are negative. If all corners of $r$ lay on one side of $l$ every dot product would be either positive or negative. Because there are one positive and three negative dot products a collision was detected.

## Rectangle-Line-Segment Collision

For this collision detection we test if the (infinite) line along the segment goes through the rectangle and if there is a horizontal or vertical separation axis. If the line collides with the rectangle and there is no axis-aligned separation axis then we have found a collision.

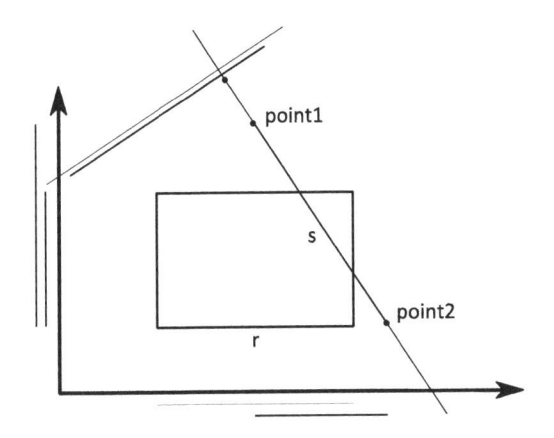

```
Bool rectangle_segment_collide(Rectangle r, Segment s)
{
    Line sLine;
    sLine.base = s.point1;
    sLine.direction = subtract_vector(s.point2, s.point1);
    if(!line_rectangle_collide(sLine, r))
        return no;

    Range rRange, sRange;
    rRange.minimum = r.origin.x;
    rRange.maximum = r.origin.x + r.size.x;
    sRange.minimum = s.point1.x;
    sRange.maximum = s.point2.x;
    sRange = sort_range(sRange);
    if(!overlapping_ranges(rRange, sRange))
        return no;

    rRange.minimum = r.origin.y;
    rRange.maximum = r.origin.y + r.size.y;
    sRange.minimum = s.point1.y;
    sRange.maximum = s.point2.y;
    sRange = sort_range(sRange);
    return overlapping_ranges(rRange, sRange);
}

Rectangle r = {{3, 2}, {6, 4}};
Segment s = {{6, 8}, {10, 2}};

assert(yes == rectangle_segment_collide(r, s));
```

The initial line collision part should be clear. The second part tests if segment and rectangle overlap when projected onto the horizontal axis. The third part tests the same on the vertical axis.

## Rectangle-Oriented-Rectangle Collision

The easiest way here would be to convert the axis-aligned rectangle into an oriented one and use function *oriented_rectangles_collide()*. But for speed's sake we use a specialized algorithm.

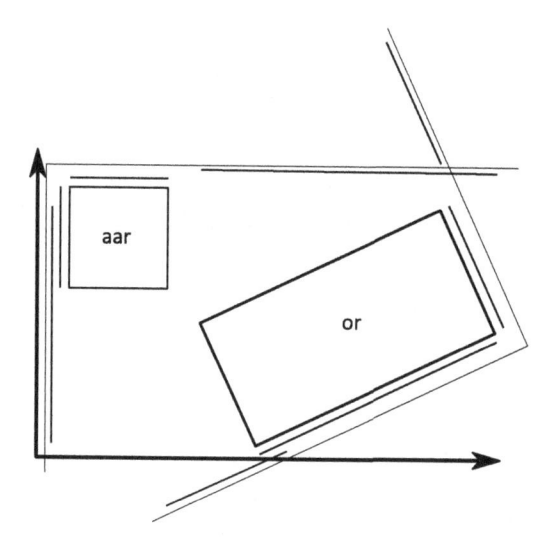

```
Vector2D rectangle_corner(Rectangle r, int nr)
{
    Vector2D corner = r.origin;
    switch(nr % 4)
    {
    case 0:
        corner.x += r.size.x;
        break;
    case 1:
        corner = add_vector(corner, r.size);
        break;
    case 2:
        corner.y += r.size.y;
        break;
    default:
        /* corner = r.origin */
        break;
    }
    return corner;
```

```
}

Bool separating_axis_for_rectangle(Segment axis, Rectangle r)
{
    Segment rEdgeA, rEdgeB;
    Range axisRange, rEdgeARange, rEdgeBRange, rProjection;
    Vector2D n = subtract_vector(axis.point1, axis.point2);

    rEdgeA.point1 = rectangle_corner(r, 0);
    rEdgeA.point2 = rectangle_corner(r, 1);
    rEdgeB.point1 = rectangle_corner(r, 2);
    rEdgeB.point2 = rectangle_corner(r, 3);
    rEdgeARange = project_segment(rEdgeA, n);
    rEdgeBRange = project_segment(rEdgeB, n);
    rProjection = range_hull(rEdgeARange, rEdgeBRange);

    axisRange = project_segment(axis, n);

    return !overlapping_ranges(axisRange, rProjection);
}

Vector2D oriented_rectangle_corner(OrientedRectangle r, int nr)
{
    Vector2D c = r.halfExtend;
    switch(nr % 4) {
        case 0:
            c.x = -c.x;
            break;
        case 1:
            /* c = r.halfExtend */
            break;
        case 2:
            c.y = -c.y;
            break;
        default:
            c = negate_vector(c);
            break;
    }

    c = rotate_vector(c, r.rotation);
    return add_vector(c, r.center);
}

float minimum(float a, float b)
{
    return a < b ? a : b;
}

float maximum(float a, float b)
{
    return a > b ? a : b;
```

```
}

Rectangle enlarge_rectangle_point(Rectangle r, Vector2D p)
{
    Rectangle enlarged;
    enlarged.origin.x = minimum(r.origin.x, p.x);
    enlarged.origin.y = minimum(r.origin.y, p.y);
    enlarged.size.x = maximum(r.origin.x + r.size.x, p.x);
    enlarged.size.y = maximum(r.origin.y + r.size.y, p.y);
    enlarged.size = subtract_vector(enlarged.size,
                                    enlarged.origin);
    return enlarged;
}

Rectangle oriented_rectangle_rectangle_hull(OrientedRectangle
r)
{
    Rectangle h = {r.center, {0, 0}};

    int nr;
    Vector2D corner;
    for(nr = 0; nr < 4; ++nr)
    {
        corner = oriented_rectangle_corner(r, nr);
        h = enlarge_rectangle_point(h, corner);
    }
    return h;
}

Bool oriented_rectangle_rectangle_collide(OrientedRectangle or,
                                          Rectangle aar)
{
    Rectangle orHull = oriented_rectangle_rectangle_hull(or);
    if(!rectangles_collide(orHull, aar))
        return no;

    Segment edge = oriented_rectangle_edge(or, 0);
    if(separating_axis_for_rectangle(edge, aar))
        return no;

    edge = oriented_rectangle_edge(or, 1);
    return !separating_axis_for_rectangle(edge, aar);
}

Rectangle aar = {{1, 5}, {3, 3}};
OrientedRectangle or = {{10, 4}, {4, 2}, 25};

assert(no == oriented_rectangle_rectangle_collide(or, aar));
```

That's quite a pile of code. Let's decompose it step by step.

We start with *oriented_rectangle_rectangle_collide()*. It's first check tests if the axis-aligned, rectangular hull of *or* intersects with *aar*. A shape's rectangular hull is the tightest rectangle which fully contains the shape:

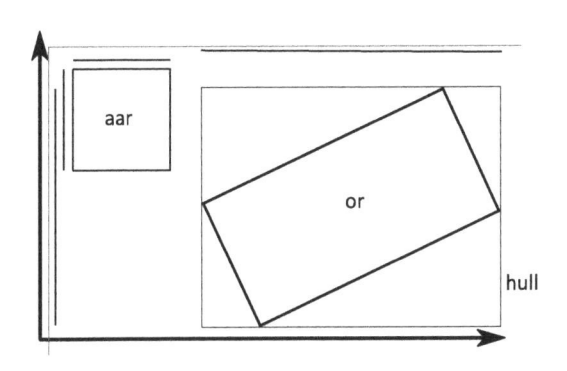

This illustration shows just the axis-aligned projections of *aar* and *or*. As you can see *or* and its *hull* have equal projections. Therefore we can use function *rectangles_collide()* to test if the projections overlap. In this case they overlap only on the vertical axis.

Function *oriented_rectangle_rectangle_hull()* returns the hull for the oriented rectangle. For this computation we create a hull rectangle and enlarge it with all four corners of the oriented rectangle. Function *enlarge_rectangle_point()* is used for enlarging. It takes a rectangle, extends it as little as possible to cover the point and returns this new, possibly larger rectangle.

The two functions *oriented_rectangle_corner()* and *rectangle_corner()* do the same as each other. They return the specified corner point of a rectangle. The difference is just that the former function takes an oriented rectangle while the latter takes an axis-aligned one. It's not defined which corner will be returned for which number. It's only guaranteed that adjacent numbers correspond to corners which share a common edge. For example, corners for numbers 0 and 1 are the end points of one edge. The same is true for combinations 1-2, 2-3 and 3-0.

Finally, in the second and third tests of *oriented_rectangle_rectangle_collide()*, function *separating_axis_for_rectangle()* is the axis-aligned equivalent of *separating_axis_for_oriented_rectangle()*. It takes a *Rectangle* instead of an *OrientedRectangle* as parameter. Check out section Oriented-Rectangle-Oriented-Rectangle Collision for details on the inner workings of *separating_axis_for_oriented_rectangle()*.

## Point-Line Collision

When a point collides with a line it means the point must lie on the line.

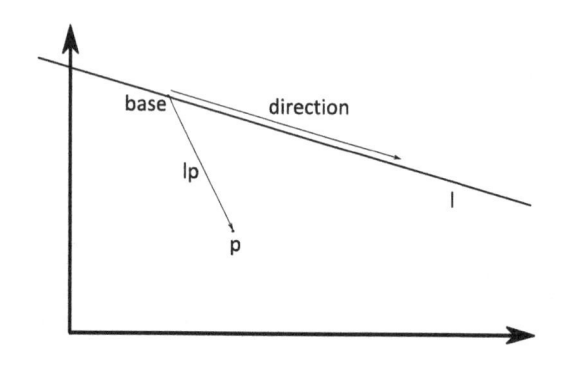

```
Bool line_point_collide(Line l, Vector2D p)
{
    if(points_collide(l.base, p))
        return yes;

    Vector2D lp = subtract_vector(p, l.base);
    return parallel_vectors(lp, l.direction);
}

Vector2D p = {5, 3};
Line l = {{3, 7}, {7, -2}};

assert(no == line_point_collide(l, p));
```

The code is rather simple. First we test if *p* lies on the line's base. If that's the case we have found a collision. Otherwise we compute *lp* which is the distance from *base* to *p*. When *lp* and the line's *direction* are parallel, point *p* must lie on line *l*.

## Point-Line-Segment Collision

This algorithm is nearly equivalent to circle-line-segment collision detection, just without a radius.

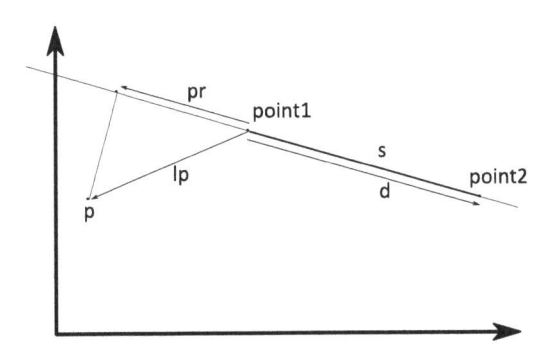

```
Bool point_segment_collide(Vector2D p, Segment s)
{
    Vector2D d = subtract_vector(s.point2, s.point1);
    Vector2D lp = subtract_vector(p, s.point1);
    Vector2D pr = project_vector(lp, d);
    return equal_vectors(lp, pr)
           &&
           vector_length(pr) <= vector_length(d)
           &&
           0 <= dot_product(pr, d);
}

Vector2D p = {1, 4};
Segment s = {{6, 6}, {13, 4}};

assert(no == point_segment_collide(p, s));
```

When *lp* and *pr* are equal, point *p* lies at least on the endless line going through segment *s*. If so, we have to find out if *p* lies between the segment end points. This is done by testing if *pr* is shorter than the segment's length and if *pr* and *d* point in the same direction. A negative dot product means opposing vectors in this case.

## Point-Oriented-Rectangle Collision

Analogous to circle-oriented-rectangle collision detection we simply transform the point into the rectangle's local coordinate system and use the function already explained *point_rectangle_collide()*.

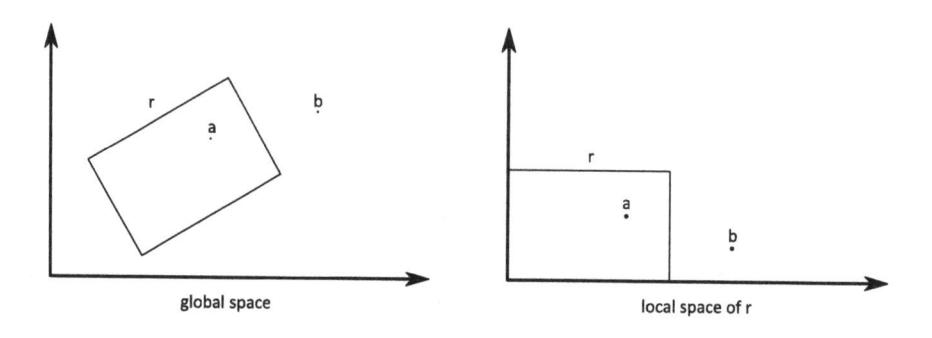

global space

local space of r

```
Bool oriented_rectangle_point_collide(OrientedRectangle r,
                                      Vector2D p)
{
    Rectangle lr;
    lr.origin.x = 0;
    lr.origin.y = 0;
    lr.size = multiply_vector(r.halfExtend, 2);

    Vector2D lp = subtract_vector(p, r.center);
    lp = rotate_vector(lp, -r.rotation);
    lp = add_vector(lp, r.halfExtend);

    return point_rectangle_collide(lp, lr);
}
OrientedRectangle r = {{5, 4}, {3, 2}, 30};
Vector2D a = {6, 5};
Vector2D b = {10, 6};

assert(yes == oriented_rectangle_point_collide(r, a));
assert(no == oriented_rectangle_point_collide(r, b));
```

## Line-Line-Segment Collision

To find out if a line collides with a line segment we just need to determine if the segment's end points lie on the same side of the line. If they do a collision is impossible.

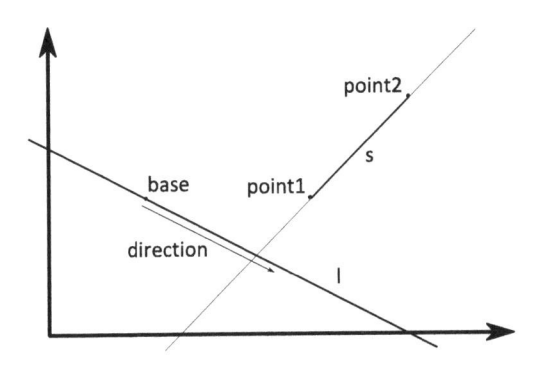

```
Bool line_segment_collide(Line l, Segment s)
{
    return !on_one_side(l, s);
}

Vector2D base = {3, 4};
Vector2D direction = {4, -2};
Vector2D point1 = {8, 4};
Vector2D point2 = {11, 7};

Segment s = {point1, point2};
Line l = {base, direction};

assert(no == line_segment_collide(l, s));
```

Function *on_one_side()* is explained in section Line-Segment-Line-Segment Collision.

## Line-Oriented-Rectangle Collision

Different shape, same trick. As done in section Circle-Oriented-Rectangle Collision Detection we employ the convert-to-local-space concept here:

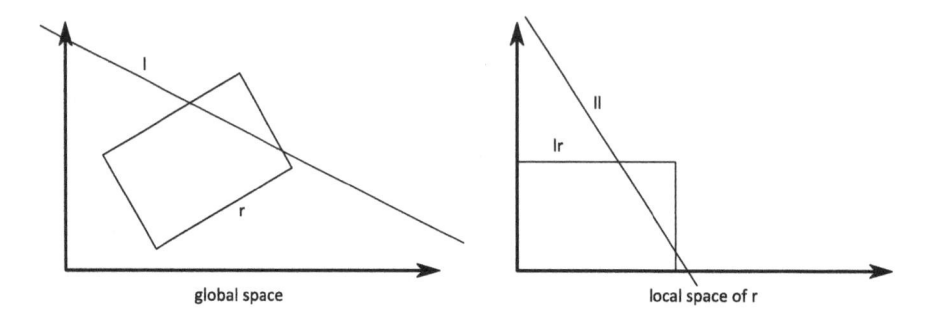

global space

local space of r

```
Bool line_oriented_rectangle_collide(Line l,
                                     OrientedRectangle r)
{
    Rectangle lr;
    lr.origin.x = 0;
    lr.origin.y = 0;
    lr.size = multiply_vector(r.halfExtend, 2);

    Line ll;
    ll.base = subtract_vector(l.base, r.center);
    ll.base = rotate_vector(ll.base, -r.rotation);
    ll.base = add_vector(ll.base, r.halfExtend);
    ll.direction = rotate_vector(l.direction, -r.rotation);

    return line_rectangle_collide(ll, lr);
}

Line l = {{7, 3}, {2, -1}};
OrientedRectangle r = {{5, 4}, {3, 2}, 30};

assert(yes == line_oriented_rectangle_collide(l, r));
```

## Line-Segment-Oriented-Rectangle Collision

This is the same algorithm as used for line-oriented-rectangle collision detection. The difference is that we have a line segment instead of an infinite line.

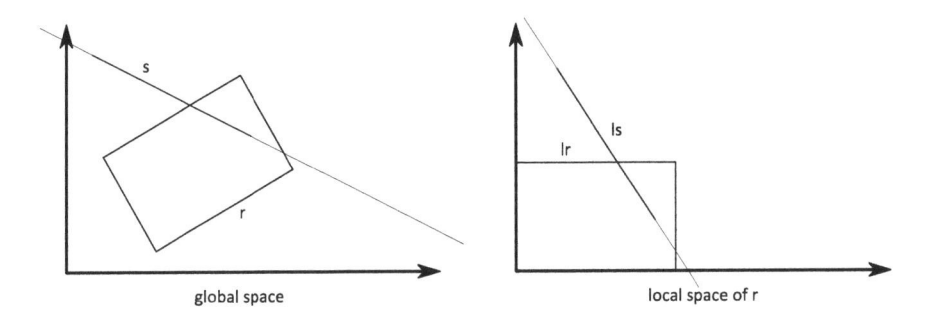

global space

local space of r

```
Bool oriented_rectangle_segment_collide(OrientedRectangle r,
                                        Segment s)
{
    Rectangle lr;
    lr.origin.x = 0;
    lr.origin.y = 0;
    lr.size = multiply_vector(r.halfExtend, 2);

    Segment ls;
    ls.point1 = subtract_vector(s.point1, r.center);
    ls.point1 = rotate_vector(ls.point1, -r.rotation);
    ls.point1 = add_vector(ls.point1, r.halfExtend);
    ls.point2 = subtract_vector(s.point2, r.center);
    ls.point2 = rotate_vector(ls.point2, -r.rotation);
    ls.point2 = add_vector(ls.point2, r.halfExtend);

    return rectangle_segment_collide(lr, ls);
}

Segment s = {{1, 8}, {7, 5}};
OrientedRectangle r = {{5, 4}, {3, 2}, 30};

assert(yes == oriented_rectangle_segment_collide(r, s));
```

# Bounding Shapes

Different shapes have different collision detection functions. Depending on the shape types these functions have varying costs regarding computation time. Circles, for example, allow very fast collision detection. On the other hand testing oriented rectangles is quite slow. We are talking about a factor greater than 100. During the time it takes *oriented_rectangles_collide()* to execute once we could call *circles_collide()* more than 100 times.

Oriented rectangles are good representations for angular objects, e.g. a car in top-down perspective. The problem is that this shape type is "slow". At first glance it looks like a trade-off between accuracy and speed: should collision detection be precise or fast?

To get both benefits we can use bounding shapes:

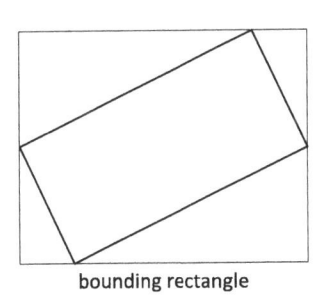

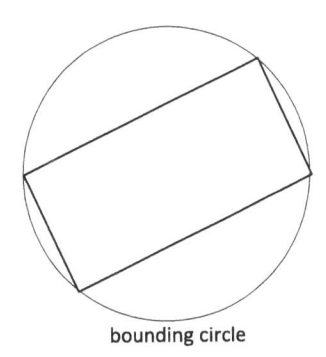

bounding rectangle

bounding circle

If we have a "slow" shape like an oriented rectangle we wrap it in a "faster" bounding shape (called a hull in code examples) like an axis-aligned rectangle or a circle. When it comes to collision detection we check the bounding shapes of both objects first. If they don't collide the enclosed shapes won't either. Otherwise we have to test the shapes for a precise result.

This may sound like a bad idea. We just doubled the number of collision detection function calls. That's true, theoretically. But collisions "rarely" occur. In most cases the objects are too far apart to collide. Think of a scenario where one game character is in town A and the other character resides in town B. They are miles apart from each other. So why waste time using a precise collision detection algorithm? This is the point where bounding shapes come into play to curtail many tests.

The following sections will show you how to compute bounding circles and bounding rectangles for different shapes.

## Bounding Rectangle

This is the code for computing the bounding rectangle for an oriented rectangle:

```
Rectangle oriented_rectangle_rectangle_hull(OrientedRectangle r)
{
    Rectangle h;
    h.origin = r.center;
    h.size.x = 0;
    h.size.y = 0;

    int nr;
    Vector2D corner;
    for(nr = 0; nr < 4; nr++)
    {
        corner = oriented_rectangle_corner(r, nr);
        h = enlarge_rectangle_point(h, corner);
    }
    return h;
}
```

The idea is to get the corner points of the oriented rectangle and find the smallest enclosing axis-aligned rectangle for them. The same concept works for finite shapes (so not for endless lines) which are defined by corner points, e.g. line segments.

## Bounding Circle

The code for computing a bounding circle for an oriented rectangle is simple:

```
Circle oriented_rectangle_circle_hull(OrientedRectangle r)
{
    Circle h;
```

```
    h.center = r.center;
    h.radius = vector_length(r.halfExtend);
    return h;
}
```

The rectangle's half extend already defines the radius for the bounding circle. The center of rectangle and circle are the same.

## Circle or Rectangle?

Up to this point we were talking about circles and rectangles as cheapest bounding shapes. Which should you decide for? The rule of thumb is:

*Use rectangles if most of your game objects won't rotate.*
*Use circles otherwise.*

The advantage of rectangles is that their collision detection is slightly faster than that of circles. On the other hand circles are immune to rotation. This means rotating an object around the bounding circle's center does not change the bounding shape. If it were a rectangle, recalculation would be necessary.

# Shape Grouping

Using a single shape per object is fine as long as it is almost rectangular or circular. For more complex objects we need multiple shapes to represent the entire body.

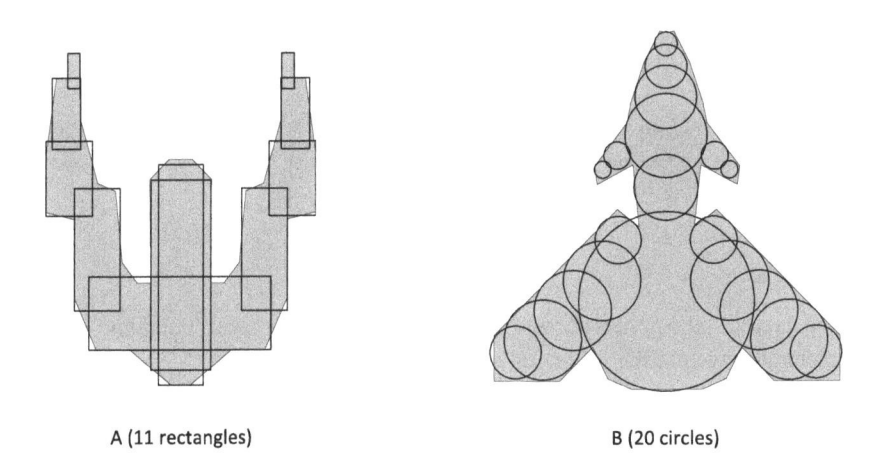

A (11 rectangles)

B (20 circles)

Now we have to deal with a set of shapes per object. To find out if two objects of such complexity collide we have to test each single shape of $A$ with each single shape of $B$. The illustrated example would result in 11 x 20 = 220 rectangle-circle tests. Because the objects don't overlap all the tests have to be performed just to find out that in the end there is no collision!

## Bounded Shape Groups

As introduced in chapter Bounding Shapes we can encapsulate shapes in bounding circles or rectangles for faster collision tests. Now we extend this concept by wrapping all the shapes of an object in one bounding shape. This way we can check the enclosing shapes of two objects first to get a fast answer on whether there is a collision.

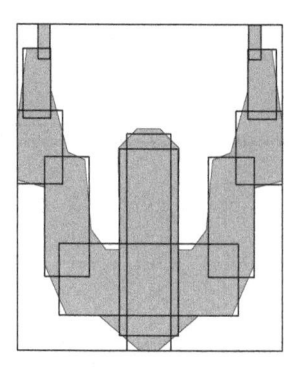

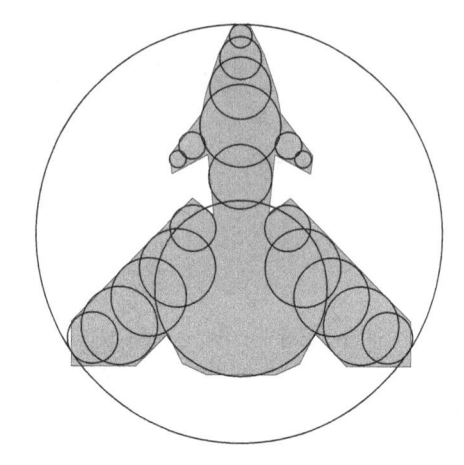

As you can see: testing the bounding shapes immediately tells us that there can't be a collision. That's 220 tests saved!

## The Code

For the example illustrated above we need to compute the group bounding shapes. For rectangles we use the following code:

```
Rectangle enlarge_rectangle_rectangle(Rectangle r,
                                      Rectangle extender)
{
    Vector2D maxCorner = add_vector(extender.origin,
                                    extender.size);
    Rectangle enlarged = enlarge_rectangle_point(r, maxCorner);
    return enlarge_rectangle_point(enlarged, extender.origin);
}

Rectangle rectangles_rectangle_hull(Rectangle* rectangles,
                                    int count)
{
    int i;
    Rectangle h = {{0, 0}, {0, 0}};
    if(0 == count)
        return h;

    h = rectangles[0];
    for(i = 1; i < count; i++)
        h = enlarge_rectangle_rectangle(h, rectangles[i]);
```

```
        return h;
}
```

Function *rectangles_rectangle_hull()* takes an array of rectangles and computes their enclosing rectangle - the hull. Function *enlarge_rectangle_rectangle()* basically does the same. It gets utilized by *rectangles_rectangle_hull()* to compute the hull of two rectangles.

After rectangles, computing a circular boundary around a set of circles looks like this:

```
Rectangle circles_rectangle_hull(Circle* circles, int count)
{
    int i;
    Vector2D halfExtend, minP, maxP;
    Rectangle h = {{0, 0}, {0, 0}};
    if(0 == count)
        return h;

    h.origin = circles[0].center;
    for(i = 0; i < count; i++)
    {
        halfExtend.x = circles[i].radius;
        halfExtend.y = circles[i].radius;
        minP = subtract_vector(circles[i].center, halfExtend);
        maxP = add_vector(circles[i].center, halfExtend);
        h = enlarge_rectangle_point(h, minP);
        h = enlarge_rectangle_point(h, maxP);
    }
    return h;
}

Vector2D rectangle_center(Rectangle r)
{
    Vector2D halfSize = divide_vector(r.size, 2);
    return add_vector(r.origin, halfSize);
}

Circle circles_circle_hull(Circle* circles, int count)
{
    int i;
    Circle h = {{0, 0}, 0};
    Rectangle rh = circles_rectangle_hull(circles, count);
    h.center = rectangle_center(rh);

    for(i = 0; i < count; i++)
    {
```

```
        Vector2D d = subtract_vector(circles[i].center,
                                     h.center);
        float extension = vector_length(d) + circles[i].radius;
        h.radius = maximum(extension, h.radius);
    }
    return h;
}
```

Function *circles_circle_hull()* first computes the hull center. For this it uses function *circles_rectangle_hull()* to compute the rectangular hull. This hull's center becomes the center for the circular hull. Afterwards we compute the radius of the smallest hull to completely enclose all circles.

---

This algorithm does not guarantee the **smallest** circle hull. In many cases smaller hulls are possible. There are more sophisticated algorithms using iterative hull shrinking or dealing with direction of maximum spread. They find better hulls but are slower and way more complex than the solution presented here.

Function *circles_circle_hull()* generates good results in most cases. So there's no need for over-engineering. Keep it simple until you have to improve.

# Shapes in Motion

So far we've talked about collisions of stationary shapes. Games have plenty of immobile objects. Examples are walls, trees or houses. But there's also a good chance for moving objects. A game without moving parts would be quite boring, wouldn't it? So we have to take movement into consideration.

## The Tunneling Problem

Games run at specific frame rates. Every frame has to be computed separately. So games are similar to cartoons which are sequences of separately crafted images. Well, they were at least in pre-CGI days.

A frame is a snapshot of a game's state at a specific time point. It tells us where the shapes are located and where they are heading at that time.

Let's check out the following situation:

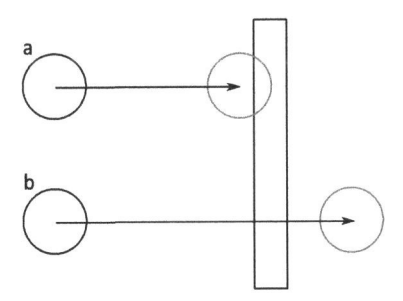

The illustration shows two balls heading in the same direction towards a rectangular obstacle. Ball *a* travels at a lower speed than ball *b*. In the first frame both balls are located at the same horizontal position, on the rectangle's left. In the next frame ball *a* collides with the obstacle while ball *b* passes through it. This effect is called tunneling.

> The probability of an object going through an obstacle unnoticed increases as its speed increases. The bigger an object is, the less it will suffer from tunneling. So the ratio of speed and size define the tunneling probability.

## Linear Impact Search

To solve the tunneling problem we can take intermediate steps into account. The brute force solution would be testing the object stepwise displaced by fractions of the full movement.

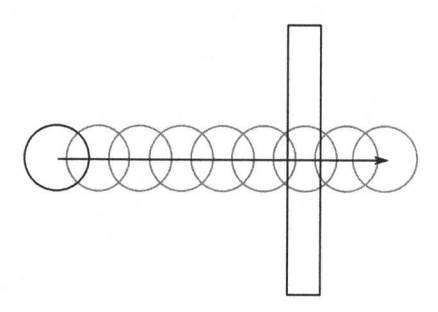

The number of tests rises proportionally with speed. This is no problem for slow objects. Whereas fast objects need many tests to avoid tunneling. Imagine a bullet fired at a wall. The high speed would result in a great number of collision tests. Now imagine a full battalion firing at that wall. The game's frame rate would start to crawl.

## Binary Impact Search

To get a better scaling algorithm we can use binary search. It starts this way:

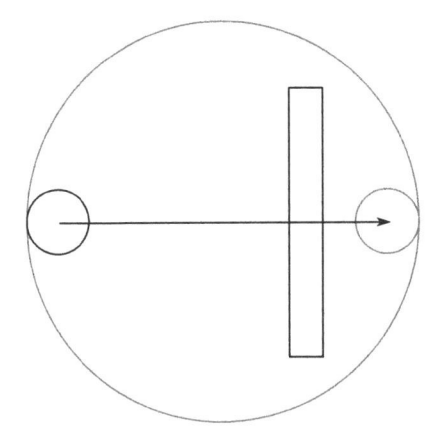

We enclose the moving object's current position and moved position in a bounding circle. If the obstacle does not collide with this bounding circle we know there can't be a collision. Otherwise we subdivide the problem into two halves:

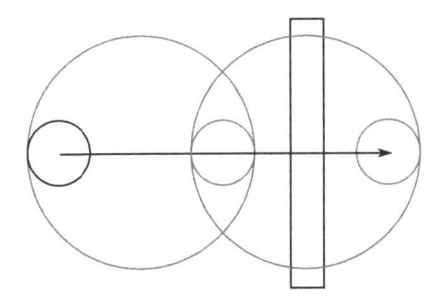

The first half represents the object covering the first half of the distance. As done before we encircle the start and end position with a bounding circle. If this bounding circle were to collide with the obstacle we would continue subdividing this movement segment. But it doesn't, so we test the second bounding circle, wrapping the halfway-through object and its destination position. This bounding circle collides with the obstacle so we subdivide the second half as done before:

collision found!

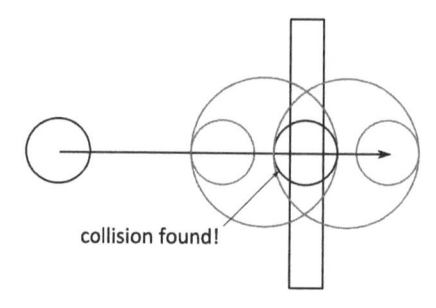

This goes on until the subdivided distance gets close to zero. How close to zero is a matter of required accuracy. The moving shape's size gives a good factor for the minimum distance.

This method is generic and works with all kinds of shapes. Tweaking the minimum distance gives us control over the trade-off between speed and accuracy. Longer distances result in faster collision detection, smaller distances yield more accurate results.

```
Bool moving_circle_rectangle_collide(Circle a,
                                     Vector2D moveA,
                                     Rectangle b)
{
    Circle envelope = a;
    Vector2D halfMoveA = divide_vector(moveA, 2);
    float moveDistance = vector_length(moveA);
    envelope.center = add_vector(a.center, halfMoveA);
    envelope.radius = a.radius + moveDistance / 2;

    if(circle_rectangle_collide(envelope, b))
    {
        float epsilon = 1.0f / 32.0f;
        float minimumMoveDistance = maximum(a.radius / 4,
                                            epsilon);
        if(moveDistance < minimumMoveDistance)
            return yes;

        envelope.radius = a.radius;
        return moving_circle_rectangle_collide(a, halfMoveA, b)
            ||
               moving_circle_rectangle_collide(envelope,
                                               halfMoveA,
```

```
                                                                    b);
        }
        else
            return no;
}
```

This function has some details which need explanation.

First there is *minimumMoveDistance*. This is the smallest distance to which the algorithm subdivides the movement. It gets derived from the moving circle's radius. Big circles need fewer tests than small ones.

Then there is *epsilon*. This is the minimum value for *minimumMoveDistance*. It's needed to prevent an endless approximation situation: when the circle's radius is zero. In this case *minimumMoveDistance* would be zero without limitation by *epsilon*. The subdivision would go on endlessly. Well, at least until the program stack exploded.

The last detail is the use of *moving_circle_rectangle_collide()* twice in the same statement. Won't it become a linear search when both halves of the movement get checked? No, because language C has short-circuit evaluation. This means that when one of the two function calls returns *yes* the other call won't be executed. Put simply: when a == yes then statement a || b is always true, regardless what b is. So b won't be evaluated.

As said before, this algorithm is generic. We can replace the circle with a rectangle and it works as well:

```
Bool moving_rectangle_rectangle_collide(Rectangle a,
                                        Vector2D moveA,
                                        Rectangle b)
{
    Rectangle envelope = a;
    envelope.origin = add_vector(envelope.origin, moveA);
    envelope = enlarge_rectangle_rectangle(envelope, a);

    if(rectangles_collide(envelope, b))
    {
        float epsilon = 1.0f / 32.0f;
        float min = minimum(a.size.x, a.size.y) / 4;
        float minimumMoveDistance = maximum(min, epsilon);
        Vector2D halfMoveA = divide_vector(moveA, 2);

        if(vector_length(moveA) < minimumMoveDistance)
            return yes;
```

```
            envelope.origin = add_vector(a.origin, halfMoveA);
            envelope.size = a.size;
            return moving_rectangle_rectangle_collide(a,
                                                     halfMoveA,
                                                     b)
                   ||
                   moving_rectangle_rectangle_collide(envelope,
                                                     halfMoveA,
                                                     b);
        }
        else
            return no;
    }
```

There is a very simple and fast collision detection algorithm when just circles are involved. Its basic idea is to reduce the moving circle to a line segment. In addition, the stationary circle gets enlarged by the moving circle's radius.

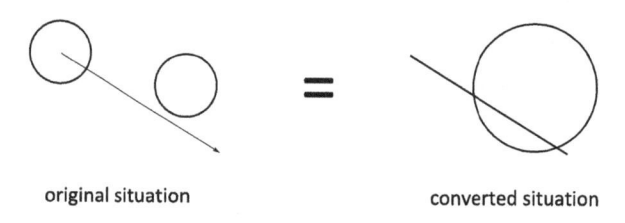

original situation          converted situation

```
    Bool moving_circle_circle_collide(Circle a,
                                      Vector2D moveA,
                                      Circle b)
    {
        Circle bAbsorbedA;
        bAbsorbedA.center = b.center;
        bAbsorbedA.radius = a.radius + b.radius;

        Segment travelA;
        travelA.point1 = a.center;
        travelA.point2 = add_vector(a.center, moveA);

        return circle_segment_collide(bAbsorbedA, travelA);
    }
```

Why does this work?

Imagine two circles touching each other. The distance between their centers equals the sum of their radii. When you shrink the radius of one circle by x and enlarge the other circle by x they still touch. Therefore shrinking circle *a* to a point (zero radius) and enlarging circle *b* by *a*'s radius gives us a point-circle collision test. When a point moves its trace resembles a line segment. So we get a line-segment-circle collision test which executes much faster than the equivalent generic binary search. And it's 100% precise. Circles rule!

## When Both Objects Move

... we can use a simple trick: we subtract the movement of object *a* from both objects' movements.

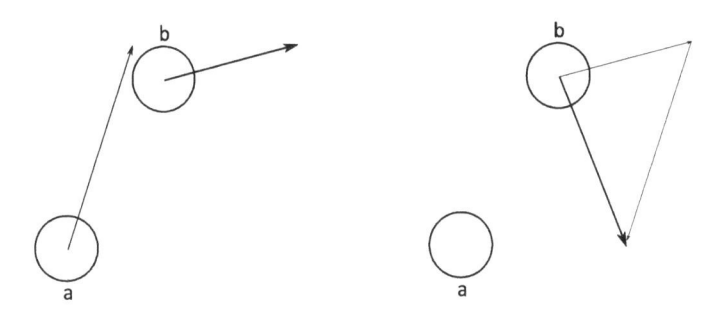

This way, object *a* remains stationary while object *b* does all the moving. Their motion relative to each other stays the same. Now we can apply the algorithms we have learned so far.

As yet we don't have a function *moving_rectangle_circle_collide()*. Instead of writing a full-blown binary search function we use the make-one-object-stationary trick from above:

```
Bool moving_rectangle_circle_collide(Rectangle a,
                                     Vector2D moveA,
                                     Circle b)
{
    Vector2D moveB = negate_vector(moveA);
    return moving_circle_rectangle_collide(b, moveB, a);
}
```

We just invert the movement of *a* and take it as movement for *b*. This way *a* becomes stationary and *b* moves. Now we can use the function already defined, *moving_circle_rectangle_collide()*.

# Optimization Tricks

One of the most challenging parts of game programming is writing fast code. This chapter presents some optimization tricks for speeding up collision detection and code in general.

Optimization is a vast, permanently changing topic. So these few tricks here are just a tiny fraction of what can be done to improve performance.

## Abstraction is King

Most game objects don't have exact circular or rectangular shapes. Therefore we need to approximate their silhouettes with multiple simple shapes. It's rarely necessary for game objects to have 100% correct shape coverage. An approximation works well in most cases.

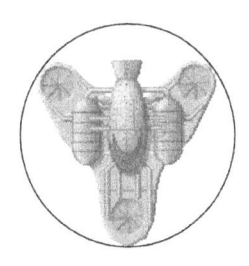

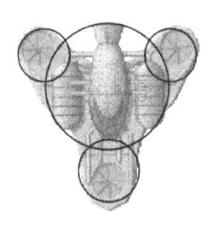

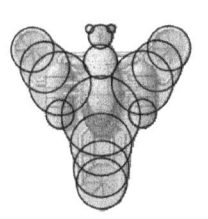

The illustration shows the same sprite abstracted with different numbers of circles. The accuracy rises to the right while collision test speed increases to the left.

## Size Matters

How big are your game objects? A sprite covering half of the screen (e.g. a level boss) demands a high collision shape accuracy. It needs plenty of shapes. On the other hand a single point can represent an object consisting of just a few pixels (e.g. a bullet).

A rule of thumb:

> *The bigger the object the more shapes.*

## Rotating by Right Angles

Trigonometric functions like *sinf()* or *cosf()* are expensive regarding computation time. Therefore function *rotate_vector()* is expensive as well. When we have right angles we can avoid using this generic function. Whenever we rotate something by a multiple of 90° (90°, 180°, 270°, etc.) we can use the following functions:

```
Vector2D rotate_vector_90(Vector2D v)
{
    Vector2D r;
    r.x = -v.y;
    r.y = v.x;
    return r;
}

Vector2D rotate_vector_180(Vector2D v)
{
    return negate_vector(v);
}

Vector2D rotate_vector_270(Vector2D v)
{
    Vector2D r;
    r.x = v.y;
    r.y = -v.x;
    return r;
}
```

Measurements have shown that the specialized functions for 90° and 270° are 2-3 times faster than their generic counterparts. Funnily enough, specializing 180° didn't bring any speed improvement. Maybe the underlying C standard library implementation handled this case already.

> The performance tests were compiled with Microsoft Visual Studio 2005®. Other compilers combined with alternative library implementations may produce different results.

Good compilers and libraries may render these specialized functions obsolete. Nevertheless you are on the safe side using them if your programming environment isn't top-notch.

## Pass Arguments by Reference

The code examples in this book pass function parameters by value. This means calling a function creates a copy of each parameter. Because most functions don't change the parameters we could pass just the addresses (pointers) of the parameters to the functions.

```
float dot_product_values(Vector2D a, Vector2D b)
{
    return a.x * b.x + a.y * b.y;
}

float dot_product_pointers(Vector2D* a, Vector2D* b)
{
    return a->x * b->x + a->y * b->y;
}

void use_dot_product_functions()
{
    Vector2D a, b;
    dot_product_values(a, b);/* copies a and b */
    dot_product_pointers(&a, &b);/* points to a and b */
}
```

This only makes sense when the parameter's size is greater than the CPU registers. For 32-bit processors this means 4 bytes, for 64-bit processors it's 8 bytes. So passing a *Vector2D* (= 2 x float = 2 x 4 bytes) by value on a 64-bit machine would last as long as passing its address. On a 32-bit machine passing a pointer would be faster than passing by value.

Calling *dot_product_values()* lasts longer than calling *dot_product_pointers()*. Good compilers may detect read-only parameters and optimize the code accordingly. When you explicitly pass parameters by pointers you will get this benefit for sure.

## Avoid Square Root

Like trigonometric functions, *sqrtf()* is a time-costly function. Avoid it whenever you can. A good example for replacing it is comparing two vector lengths.

```
Bool compare_slow(Vector2D a, Vector2D b)
{
    return vector_length(a) < vector_length(b);
}

Bool compare_fast(Vector2D a, Vector2D b)
{
    return dot_product(a) < dot_product(b);
}
```

The two functions yield the same results. The latter is faster because it does not compute any square roots. Consult section Dot Product and Vector Length for details.

## Short-Circuit Coding

The gist of this technique is: leave functions as soon as possible.

Compare function *rectangles_collide()* and its alternative *rectangles_collide_short_circuit()*:

```
Bool rectangles_collide(Rectangle a, Rectangle b)
{
    float aLeft = a.origin.x;
    float aRight = aLeft + a.size.x;
    float bLeft = b.origin.x;
    float bRight = bLeft + b.size.x;

    float aBottom = a.origin.y;
    float aTop = aBottom + a.size.y;
    float bBottom = b.origin.y;
    float bTop = bBottom + b.size.y;
```

```
    return overlapping(aLeft, aRight, bLeft, bRight)
        &&
        overlapping(aBottom, aTop, bBottom, bTop);
}

Bool rectangles_collide_short_circuit(Rectangle a, Rectangle b)
{
    float aLeft = a.origin.x;
    float bRight = b.origin.x + b.size.x;
    if(bRight < aLeft)
        return no;

    float aRight = aLeft + a.size.x;
    float bLeft = b.origin.x;
    if(aRight < bLeft)
        return no;

    float aBottom = a.origin.y;
    float bTop = b.origin.y + b.size.y;
    if(bTop < aBottom)
        return no;

    float aTop = aBottom + a.size.y;
    float bBottom = b.origin.y;
    return bBottom <= aTop;
}
```

The first function calculates all edge values in advance and tests them at the end. The second, short-circuited function computes just one pair of edge values at a time and tests it immediately. As soon as there is no possibility of the rectangles intersecting, the function returns no. This way we can save unnecessary evaluations.

> Function *rectangles_collide()* may not be the best example regarding real-life speed gain. Multi-stage instruction pipelines in processors can make short-circuiting a simple function like this worthless. This technique becomes more important when complex operations or calls to other functions can be canceled.

## Avoid Superfluous Tests

Imagine two stationary objects. They neither move nor collide. As long as neither of them starts moving it's unnecessary to test them for collision.

A third object enters the scene, heading towards the other objects. Now only the pairings including the moving object make sense to get tested. Testing the pairing of the static objects is still superfluous.

Further there is no need to test if object *b* collides with object *a* when *a* collides with *b*. This vice-versa logic sounds obvious but gets easily overlooked.

The following code shows a simple example with both optimizations in action:

```
typedef struct
{
    Bool changed;
    Vector2D velocity;
    Circle body;
} Unit;

Unit units[10];

void stop_colliding_units()
{
    int i, k;
    for(i = 0; i < 9; i++)
    {
        for(k = i + 1; k < 10; k++)
        {
            if(units[i].changed || units[k].changed)
            {
                if(circles_collide(units[i].body,
                                   units[k].body))
                {
                    Vector2D noVelocity = {0, 0};
                    units[i].velocity = noVelocity;
                    units[k].velocity = noVelocity;
                }
            }
        }
    }
}

void move_units(float secondsGoneBy)
{
    Vector2D noVelocity = {0, 0};
    int i;
```

```
    for(i = 0; i < 10; i++)
    {
        if(equal_vectors(noVelocity, units[i].velocity))
            units[i].changed = no;
        else
        {
            Vector2D center = units[i].body.center;
            Vector2D move = units[i].velocity;
            move = multiply_vector(move, secondsGoneBy);
            units[i].body.center = add_vector(move, center);
        }
    }
}

void update_units(float secondsGoneBy)
{
    move_units(secondsGoneBy);
    stop_colliding_units();
}
```

The units are randomly moving ... things. Imagine them as billiard balls if you want.

Function *move_units()* measures the time elapsed since the last frame. It updates all unit positions according to their velocities. Units without velocity get flagged as "not changed".

Function *stop_colliding_units()* implements both optimizations mentioned above. Check out the two nested for-loops. The simplest implementation would be having both loops running over all units. This would result in 10 x 10 = 100 tests. To get rid of redundant tests we reduce the outer loop to go from 0 to 8 while the inner loop goes over all indices greater than variable *i*. This results in 9 + 8 + 7 + ... + 1 = 45 tests. That's 55% work saved.

The other optimization is checking flag *changed*. When neither of the two objects has changed since the last frame there is not need to check them for collision.

## Level of Detail

Collision tests outside the screen can be simplified. E.g. by testing only the boundary shapes of objects. If they collide it can be interpreted as if the enclosed shapes would collide. This will result in false positives, destroying battle ships which are close but not colliding.

What the heck! Nobody will ever know.

# Appendix: The Code

All code in this book can be downloaded as a zip archive containing all source code files. If you don't have a zip archive tool try the free 7-zip: *www.7-zip.org* It's available for Windows, Linux and has many ports for other platforms like Mac OS X, AIX and even Amiga.

If you compare the download code with the book code snippets you may recognize that they are different. This is because the download code was written and tested first. Then it was copied to the book and adapted for readability and understanding.

The code was written and tested with Microsoft Visual Studio 2005®. It was done keeping close to the ancient C89 standard to make the code as compatible as possible. Drop me a line at *thomas@collisiondetection2d.net* if you encounter problems during compilation. I'm always curious about details breaking meant-to-be-portable code.

## Download the code:

*www.collisiondetection2d.net/cd2d_code.zip*

# About the Author

Thomas Schwarzl is a game designer, developer, book author and digital artist wannabe.

Writing computer games since 2001 let him acquire quite some knowledge about their inner workings. Now the time has come to share the lessons learned with other developers. Thomas is working in several game development areas like programming, game design, 2D graphics and 3D modeling. But by far his favorite occupation is cranking out code while sipping steaming coffee.

He resides in the Alps, right in the heart of Austria. It's a nice place there, covered by green forests, surrounded by high mountains. The perfect place for writing games and books.

Thomas also wrote *Game Project Completed*\*, a book about how successful indie game developers finish their projects. This book does not show you how to make games. It shows you how to take your game project to the finish line. Many projects never get completed. *Game Project Completed* gives you the skills to see your game through to the finish.

From time to time Thomas dumps his insights and thoughts about game development at *www.blackgolem.com*. Feel free to come by or drop him a line at *thomas@blackgolem.com*. Messages from readers are always welcome.

\* *www.amazon.com/dp/B00INF6MGA*

Made in the USA
Columbia, SC
02 March 2018